Travel Takeaways

Julie Watson is a retired university teacher and Fellow Emeritus, who now lives on the Isle of Wight. She is the author of two books. The most recent is *Travel Takeaways*, a collection of stories from her travels around the world. When not writing she spends her time kayaking on the western Yar, wildlife watching and teaching refugees. She lives with a feline companion called Marmite.

First published by

Beachy Books in 2023

(an imprint of Beachy Books Limited)

www.beachybooks.com

1

Some of these stories first appeared in a previous Beachy Books publication called *Travel Mementos: Personal Stories about Faraway Places* © 2021 Julie Watson: Rights of Passage, Table Manners for Eating Noodles, Gelato—As It Once Was, The Dance of the Scorpions, Travels in the Company of P38, Displaced on the Spanish Plain, Where Europe Ends, Blushing Onions and Therapy by the Sea, Lovestruck in Leningrad, Seeing Red in the Canary Islands, A Hitchhiker's Guide to the Bay of Biscay, A Ride into the Shadow Underworld, The Mystery of a Nudge in the Night, Birdsong, The Misadventure of a Goose, A Long Shot and Senior Moments in Segovia.

Paperback ISBN: 9781913894085   eBook ISBN: 9781913894139

Set in Adobe Caslon Pro

Travel Takeaways

Around the World
in Forty Tales

Julie Watson

BEACHY BOOKS

In memory of my parents

Contents

When a traveller returneth home, let him not leave the countries where he hath travelled behind him.

Francis Bacon from 'Of Travel' (1625)

Introduction

I like to think that I discovered travel in 1974 when I made my first independent trip as an unworldly eighteen-year-old to work as a waitress in the French Alps—a story that is included in this collection. But the seed of my passion for travel was really planted much earlier in my childhood by a picture book, its title long forgotten but one that transported its young readers around the world through colourful maps of faraway places and pictures of the different people who lived there. This piqued my curiosity, and, since that time, I have always loved to read about other peoples' travels and later to do it myself. Travel offers a window of opportunity to experience not only what is new and unfamiliar in the world but also to learn about oneself in that world.

When I first began writing these travel memoirs I had no plan to publish them as a collection. Then, I found myself living through a time in which travel suddenly became more difficult. So, while the pandemic raged, I opted to stay home instead and substituted travelling with writing about it. And in the process, I found a new pleasure: one which combined being an armchair traveller reliving past adventures with becoming a writer. On this new journey I set out to capture in words the essential elements of time, place and encounter from my own past travel adventures. I wrote each tale in a compressed form, distilling the elements as I remembered them into a short story, or kind of vignette. These vignettes have helped me to find a writing voice.

In the writing of them, memory followed memory, and before too long I had a stockpile of travel stories. The complete collection is called *Travel Takeaways*. I chose this title because they represent my own travel recollections, reassembled into stories from those vivid and often fragmented memories that all of us take away from our most treasured travel experiences.

This book merges some stories from a tentative small collection, *Travel Mementos*, first published in 2021, with many new tales from different countries around the world. There are forty stories in all, from locations as diverse as an Italian family vineyard, a 'haunted' youth hostel in Crete, a cactus landscape beside a Mexican reservoir, and a Cold War borderland in central Europe. I have arranged the stories in groups, each with a shared theme. There are also maps showing the countries and places where my 'takeaways' are from, to help you better navigate around the world.

In scope, I hope there is something to interest everyone, whether it is an encounter with an oracle-spouting Turkish carpet vendor, a face-to-face meeting with a great ape in Borneo or a cultural blunder in a Japanese noodle restaurant. There is much more besides.

As the stories are not in chronological or geographical order, but grouped roughly according to theme, it is not important where you start. You can travel around the world taking any route you like from the comfort of your own armchair! However you choose to read my travel takeaways, I hope you enjoy them.

Julie Watson

List of stories with their geographical locations:

In the Italian Thick of It (Zagarolo, Lazio province, Italy)
Catching up with Relatives (Sandakan, Northern Sabah, Borneo)
How I Met Your Father (Istanbul, Turkey)
Beware of Vipers! (Chamrousse, The French Alps, France)
The Reluctant Climber (Mount Kinabalu, Malaysian State of Sabah, Borneo)
Seeing Red in the Canary Islands (Gran Canaria, Spain)
Mix-Mix to Go (Lombok island, Indonesia)
A Taste of French Cake (Paris and Illiers, France)
Lessons in English for Gastronomic Purposes (Gili Islands, Lombok, Indonesia)
Gelato—As It Once Was (Milan, Italy)
Table Manners for Eating Noodles (Japan)
Blushing Onions and Therapy by the Sea (Roscoff, Brittany, France)
Something to Write Home About (Taman Negara National Park, Malaysia)

A Ride into the Shadow Underworld (Jogjakarta, Indonesia)

Night Fright (Ayios Nikolaos, Crete)

A Walk on the Wild Side (Maremma, Tuscany, Italy)

Borderland (Bavarian and Bohemian Forests, Germany/Czech Republic)

A Case of Fishy Synchronicity (Shimonoseki, Busan and Seoul, Japan and South Korea)

Footloose in the Jungle (Labi to Marudi, Brunei and Sarawak, Borneo)

A Hitchhiker's Guide to the Bay of Biscay (Atlantic Ocean, west of France and north of Spain)

Travels in the Company of P38 (Israel and Egypt)

Rights of Passage (Tarifa, southern Spain)

A Long Shot (Java, Indonesia)

The Dance of the Scorpions (Durango, Mexico)

Tongue-tied in the Land of Magyars (Budapest and Székesfehérvár, Hungary)

Where Europe Ends (northern Norway)

Displaced on the Spanish Plain (Avila, Spain)

The Lure of a Landscape (Francisco Zarco Dam, Durango state, Mexico)

The Arrival (Santa Rosa National Park, Pacific coast of Costa Rica)

Mischievous Gods and a Serpentine Tangle (Mount Olympus and Lake Kerkini, Northern Greece)

The Misadventure of a Goose (Walsingham, Norfolk, England)

Lovestruck in Leningrad (St Petersburg, Russia)

The Mystery of a Nudge in the Night (Arctic Circle, Norway)
31 (Rome, Italy)
The Last Wood Turner (Toledo, Spain)
On Crocodile Beach (Brunei, Borneo)
Oracle (Didim, Aegean coast of Turkey)
Musical Postcards from India (Delhi to Bombay, India)
Birdsong (Rome, Italy)
Senior Moments in Segovia (Spain)

First Encounters

In the Italian Thick of It

'Got a busy day?' Gayle, my American housemate, asks as we sit facing each other across the breakfast table, our hands wrapped around warm mugs of café latte.

I shrug. 'No. Nothing special. Why?' The weekend has finally arrived. It's been an eventful first week of teaching at a school in Rome; five days in at the deep end. I'm feeling disorientated as well as physically shattered.

It's early autumn and I'm in a rented villa somewhere in the hinterland of Lazio province after spending my first few nights in the Italian capital, some thirty-four kilometres away. Getting off the airport bus, I walked into the first pensione that I could find in the streets behind Stazione di Termini, Rome's central railway station, and paid for a room for a week. The neighbourhood was buzzing with life during the day and, as I later discovered, at night too. It was the red-light district.

Yet, each time I ventured out of my temporary accommodation, I felt like an extra walking onto a crowded Fellini filmset where I didn't belong. I was a newly arrived alien, speaking very little Italian and living in a bubble, separated from everything around me.

The neighbourhood was bursting with activity. Wall-to-wall diners ate, talked and laughed loudly late into the night in the trattorias. Music and clientele oozed together from the bustling bars out onto the street. Only I was silent on the top floor of my pensione.

My surroundings ensured that sleep was impossible until the small hours. And on the night when the rumbling garbage truck made its weekly collection at 3 a.m. I was treated to a final serenade of screeching metal embellished with loud clatters. That night I remained awake until dawn. My aching eyes were still open when I heard the bar shutters being raised at 7 a.m.

A fellow teacher has come to my rescue. Gayle is renting a sprawling villa in Zagarolo, a small provincial town to the east, thirty minutes away on the commuter train. She has offered me a room until I can find a studio apartment to rent in Rome itself. It's a relief to get out of the pensione, but the station stop, although close to the rented villa, is some distance from Zagarolo's centre. The quietness comes as a shock after the chaos of central Rome. But I'm wondering where all the other residents are.

Gayle's voice ushers me back to the present. She and I have hardly crossed paths since I moved in. Our teaching timetables have conspired to ensure we never meet. Breakfast this morning is our first encounter as housemates.

'It's the vendemmia,' she continues and then pauses, waiting for my reaction. I look at her blankly. My Italian vocabulary threshold is still lingering on page six of the Italian phrasebook that I read on the daily commuting journey in and out of the metropolis.

'We're invited over to the vigneto—the Loreti family vineyard.'

'The farm across the road?' I'm uncertain what this implies but don't wish to appear ungracious so agree, 'Oh, good. That sounds interesting.'

We cross the road after breakfast. I've already had several near-miss encounters navigating the Roman traffic, so my head automatically swivels in all directions first. It's a safety check that is unnecessary. I haven't actually seen a single vehicle pass here since my arrival. Despite being mid-morning, a hush lies over the neighbouring villas and they still have all their shutters down.

Yet, at one time a tailback of human traffic stretched through this municipality. It was part of a noisy medieval thoroughfare that ran down through Europe and beyond. Known as the Via Francigena, it was the ancient route trodden by pilgrims coming to Rome and the Holy See from the far-flung corners of northern Christendom. After Rome those equipped with sufficient religious zeal and shoe leather would continue south to the ports of Apulia. There at Italy's heel they boarded ships bound for the Holy Land itself. Modern day Zagarolo, in contrast, seems to have lost its zest for life.

Across the road, a lush green thicket comes into view. The Vigneto Loreti. Grapevines, their sinewy arms intertwined, are rising up to march over the hillside like a compact Roman legion in row upon row of leafy helmets. The air that hangs over them stretches out fragrant fingers to tickle our noses with the musty smell of crushed grapes.

As we draw nearer, I can hear voices coming from somewhere. Emerging from within the green curtain, a straw hat appears. Next, a flash of red tee shirt. Then a blurred snapshot of a moving arm. And there, a raised hand with a pair of secateurs attached. Disconnected body parts present themselves in a photomontage. People, at last! So, this is where the Zagarolesi have been hiding. Concealed within the rows of vines there is an army of pickers: friends, family and neighbours. Half of the town's inhabitants must be here. It's the annual grape harvest (vendemmia), and we are here to join the workforce.

We are greeted effusively by one of the Loreti sons. Stocky and sun-bronzed, the young farmer drops the basket he is carrying and brushes a fringe of black curls from his brow to reveal a pair of irresistible smiling eyes. Then he directs us into the narrow space between two rows of vines where someone else hands us secateurs and a basket, and shows us how to harvest. First, by taking a bunch of grapes loosely in one hand, supporting the cluster, and then neatly snipping the stem with the secateurs. We set to work.

We are still snipping our way along the row some two hours later. Behind us is a line of brimming baskets marking our progress. They are filled with sweet red grapes, straining to escape their dusky skins. I am reaching for a new basket when a metallic jangle rings out from the farmhouse. A bucket, or some other makeshift dinner gong, is being struck loudly. Before the last clang dies away, a singing voice calls out. I catch one word: 'pranzo'. It's lunchtime. The pickers lay down their tools and we follow them inside.

In the house, the pasta is dressed in its finest sauce, wafting its scent to welcome us. An enticing smell, which, at first, I mistake for bacon. But I'm wrong. It's the more subtle aroma of pancetta, Italian dry-cured pork and a favourite ingredient in Roman cuisine. In a room adjoining the kitchen, a long wooden table with benches on either side has been laid ready with pasta dishes, cutlery and simple glass tumblers.

There is some playful commotion while everyone finds a place on a bench and clambers in. And then la Mamma Loreti arrives to an eruption of shouts and hand-clapping. She leads a procession of her kitchen aides all bearing giant bowls of pasta. Five large bowls of spaghetti carbonara are placed at intervals along the middle of the table.

There is no formality. We are supposed to help ourselves, it seems, and there is more light-hearted banter as neighbour encourages neighbour to serve themselves first. To break the impasse someone starts to lift out long tumbling tresses of spaghetti dripping with carbonara sauce and deposits them into their neighbour's dish. Soon everyone on both sides of the table has been served. Black pepper mills and plates heaped with freshly grated pecorino cheese are being passed along the benches from hand to hand. There is much grinding and liberal sprinkling over our bowls. The noise of laughter, raised voices and clinking tableware subsides a little as people begin to eat.

'Un bicchiere di vino?' My neighbour is extending a carafe of garnet-red wine towards me. I lift the glass tumbler in front of me and it is immediately filled with vino della casa. Taking a sip, I look around the table at my fellow grape pickers absorbed in animated conversation over their food. My neighbour is filling his own glass but continues talking to me. I haven't a clue what he is saying, but it doesn't matter. I smile and raise my glass. I feel part of it now and no longer like the filmset extra.

See Italy map on page 240.

Catching up with Relatives

The sweat droplets fly off me as I half run, half stumble through the saturated rainforest, berating myself. What an idiot I am to forget about my backpack! I am in the Malaysian state of Sabah in northern Borneo and the end of 1990 is fast approaching. A desire to see different parts of Borneo has brought me here from neighbouring Brunei, which has been my work base for the past few months. But I am also in Sabah because of the opportunity it presents to visit some distant cousins.

Yesterday my backpack and I were deposited at the edge of the small town of Sandakan, after a gruelling five-hour journey in the back of what the locals called a 'bas mini'. It was a twelve-seater, but one which uncomfortably accommodates up to fifteen passengers in this part of the world. Squashed into its hot sweat-scented interior, with windows wide open, we bounced and jolted our way on the vehicle's protesting suspension, along a network of potholed dirt roads. The journey would take us from the southern capital of 'KK', as everyone calls Kota Kinabalu, to Sandakan over 300 kilometres to the north.

Outside KK there were no road signs, and our route was lined with dense secondary rainforest. Displaying knowledge that would impress even a London cabbie, our driver navigated his way without a moment's hesitation. Perhaps he had his own mental map or used special tree identification skills, but, somehow, he deciphered all the esoteric signposts in the landscape, enabling him to tell the right dirt road from among a myriad of others.

The recent heavy tropical rains had taken their toll and deep mud-filled ruts, for which the minibus was ill-prepared, brought us to a standstill several times. When this happened, the stationary bus would disgorge us all into the hot sun, clutching our water bottles.

A wiry Malaysian boy then jumped out to perform one of three duties. Besides collecting fares and hanging out of the window to alert the driver of approaching potholes, he—and anyone else willing to take a mud shower—would push and shove at the rear end of the bus to release it from one of the numerous ruts. After much engine revving and pushing, the driver eventually succeeded in jerking the vehicle out. We climbed inside again, drove on and eventually arrived in Sandakan.

The next day I checked out of the Coconut Dream Hostel, where I had spent the night, and boarded another packed minibus heading out along the main road. Half an hour later, we arrived at a small intersection where I squeezed my way out. A track led off towards my destination. It was already close to 3 p.m., the time of my appointment, so I set off quickly.

The entrance was marked by a simple wooden sign greeting me in Malay: Selamat Datang (Welcome). As there didn't appear to be anybody about, I walked towards a cluster of low, green-roofed buildings. Nothing indicated that this was the rehabilitation centre I was seeking, but there was an open door to one of them, so I entered. Inside, I found a receptionist waiting. Yes, he confirmed, after signing me in, I was a bit late, but if I hurried, I would still be in time

'Please, backpack—put in locker,' he added as I turned to leave. I was anxious to catch up with the other visitors.

Outside, another khaki-clad member of staff materialised from a matching bush. He blended so well with his olive-green surroundings that I almost missed him until he spoke. He greeted me and then pointed ahead where I could see the last of a straggling line of people disappearing between the trees into Kabili Sepilok Forest Reserve. I would catch them if I walked quickly, but, just as I reached the edge of the forest, I realised I still had my backpack stickily attached to my back.

This was a mistake that could have regrettable consequences. A story had been circulating on the backpacker's grapevine. It concerned an unsuspecting German tourist who had attracted the attention of one of the centre's residents a few weeks earlier. He had been approached and, under protest, dispossessed of his backpack. The curious resident had then climbed a nearby tree with it. The contents were carefully examined; an expensive zoom lens was forcibly pulled off an equally costly camera body. Neither part was found to conceal anything edible and so, with some disappointment, they were dropped from a considerable height.

Remembering this, I turned and retraced my steps to the reception, found an empty locker and relieved myself of my backpack. Although I had an appointment to meet one of the local residents, I didn't want any trouble.

The resident I was visiting was a 'person of the forest', more usually known by its Malay name of orangutan. And—a distant cousin. Among the great apes, this intelligent and gentle-faced primate, with shaggy red hair and monk-like face, can claim to be one of our closest relations, since humankind and orangutans are descended from a common ancestor. These cousins may well view the connection with our species with some dismay, having suffered a significant loss of habitat through recent human incursions. But we can proudly claim to share more of our physical traits with them than with either chimpanzees or gorillas. And, like orangutans, we laugh when tickled and our similar facial expressions cause onlookers to laugh as well. Adults of their species are mostly solitary, but research has shown that like their human relatives they also have the ability to recognise each other's faces, even after long periods of separation.

The Sepilok Rehabilitation Centre, where I have come, provides both a home and medical care for young, orphaned and confiscated orangutans that have been the victims of illegal logging, deforestation or the illegal pet trade. Eventually, most are rehabilitated into the surrounding forest where they are free to return to the wild, or quite literally hang around for a while to benefit from free daily handouts at one of the feeding platforms.

I stop on the path to catch my breath and drip some more sweat. The visitor group must have already reached the viewing platform by now to watch the mid-afternoon feeding session.

They are nowhere in sight. A confusing network of paths in front of me raises my anxiety level; that and an information leaflet I am clutching in my clammy hand in which I read that 'Visitors are restricted to walkways and are not allowed to approach or handle the apes. They can be dangerous.'

As this warning sinks in, breaking through the constant radio crackle of a million rainforest insects competing for an airwave, I hear the snap of a branch behind me. I turn my head and there, waddling purposefully towards me, is a female orangutan with a small baby hanging from her distended belly. Her soft brown eyes meet my startled blue ones in a long moment of mutual recognition.

No, we have not met before. Yet, standing just a few feet apart in a remote patch of tropical rainforest, each of us knows that we are being appraised by an intelligent creature similar to ourselves. It is an unexpected eye-locking moment that seems to last an eternity. Even the forest buzz surrounding us recedes into silence as two distant cousins gaze in wonder.

Then surprise changes to fear, and one of us panics—me! I stride on, quickening my pace and hoping that the mother, encumbered by her infant, will not chase me. Around the next bend in the path, the first of several feeding platforms comes into view. I look behind me, but the female and her baby are nowhere in sight.

The guide and other visitors are gathered beneath the platform, watching some juveniles as they swing in from the nearby trees. There is no fighting as the giant apes gently reach out in turn to take a ripe banana, a piece of chopped mango or a chunk of juicy red watermelon.

Soon the deck is littered with banana skins and the marbled red-green skins of the watermelon, sucked clean. The centre staff call to the orangutans by name, handing out fruit to the more hesitant or timid individuals. They are wild here, living free in the forest and fending largely for themselves, but still they remember the friendly faces of their former carers and respond to them with warm liquid eyes. It is a moving sight.

Afterwards, I return to the centre and pass the intersection where the female orangutan with her baby had approached me. I am a little ashamed of my reaction. In a moment of self-awareness, I see myself standing again on the path: an insecure member of the human species, all too easily alarmed when removed from its familiar urban territory. I feared the worst would happen, even though it is my kind which has the more dangerous track record. She probably only wanted to see if I might have a banana to spare. But my bananas are in my backpack, safely stored in the locker along with my camera. Still, I am glad that our paths crossed and that we shared that special moment of personal contact, however briefly. After all, we are related.

See Borneo and East Malaysia map on page 242.

How I Met Your Father

'Where are you going?' Oh no, here we go again. I walk faster, but he skips along beside me in the sweltering heat and dust of Istanbul and persists with his questions: 'Where are you from?' It's impossible to shake him off.

I've come to Turkey for three months, on a working holiday, and, for the first part, I'm staying with a well-heeled Turkish family in Kadıköy. It's a residential district of Istanbul on the eastern side of the Bosphorus, the narrow strait of water that separates Asia from Europe. A one month assignment as a live-in English tutor for two teenage girls sounded ideal, but it only took a couple of days before they had exhausted all ideas of what to do with me.

On day two, with an older male cousin acting as our chauffeur-cum-chaperon, I was whisked around the main tourist sights: the great Byzantine basilica of Hagia Sophia; Sultanahmet, the beautiful Blue Mosque; and Topkapi, the lavish sultan's palace. This tour was followed by a public appearance at a trendy eating place where all their teenage Turkish friends hung out.

After that the novelty wore off, and I also discovered they were less than keen to spend their precious holiday time studying

English. One lesson sufficed for us all to realise that it simply wasn't going to work. We didn't repeat the exercise but have instead reached an unspoken agreement. English lessons have been suspended until further notice. So, while they stay home, watching rented movies and experimenting with new shades of nail polish, I go out and explore the rest of Istanbul on my own.

After breakfast I make the short commute across the brown swirling waters of the Bosphorus, on one of the many ferries criss-crossing this crowded channel. I feel rather glamorous sailing back and forth from one continent to another on a daily basis.

From Kadıköy to Eminönü on the European side, up on the top deck, with a warm breeze ruffling my hair, I lean over the rail and minaret-spot, counting six for the blue mosque, four for Hagia Sophia and several belonging to other mosques, yet to be identified. Then the ferry docks, its passengers spill out and I set off on foot towards Taksim Square—the beating heart of the west bank of Istanbul, from which, arteries pump out traffic and people in all directions.

I choose the quieter backstreets to reach the square, but, somehow, my assailants know I'm coming. Like hungry gulls homing in on a discarded sandwich, they take turns to dive-bomb me, their efforts to engage me in conversation exploding on the pavement around me. Unwanted attention seems to be what I must expect as a lone foreign female on an Istanbul street.

This morning is no exception. I keep my answers as mono-syllabic as possible, not wishing to be rude and hoping he will get the message, but he's like superglue. And the questions keep on coming: 'How long have you been here? Are you staying in Eminönü?'

Suddenly, I realise that something is different today, compared to all previous days: his English. There is an accent—although perhaps not a Turkish one—but, curiously, he speaks in full sentences and ones which are grammatically correct. Perhaps this one is of a higher calibre than the usual street suitors I attract. Surprised, I stop and turn to assess the young boy beside me. Seventeen? No, a bit older, nineteen or twenty maybe. Dark hair, matching eyes, with that olive complexion signifying someone from this part of the world, give or take a thousand-kilometre radius in any direction.

Curious, I throw a question at him: 'Where are you from?'

The answer is lobbed straight back: 'Iran, but I'm Armenian.'

A moment's hesitation, and then I relent.

A while later, sipping sweet aromatic coffee together in a side street café, and I know his story. He is Khoren from Isfahan, Iran's third biggest city. An historical city known for its stunning Islamic architecture, but also with a large and diverse ethnic community including many Christian Armenians. It's 1985 and the eight-year war between Iran and its neighbour Iraq is at its height. Soldiers have been dying in droves on both sides. Iran is resorting to unarmed child soldiers, snatched from the streets. Many other young boys are fleeing to avoid conscription. Khoren has fled here over the cold high mountains in eastern Turkey, aided by people smugglers. A hazardous and difficult journey. The first time he was unsuccessful. Caught in the night by border guards and imprisoned. His parents paid a hefty bribe to release him.

The second time he made it across. Now it's a waiting game. The UNHCR processing apparatus is slow and overwhelmed with applications for asylum. Khoren hopes to go west to the USA or Canada. It could take several years, he tells me. Some boys get tired of waiting, buy a fake passport and a one-way plane ticket. Then, once up in the sky, they tear up their papers and flush them down the toilet, claiming asylum on arrival at their destination.

Khoren is articulate and appears calm, despite his precarious situation: resigned to waiting patiently. He tells me about his love of classical music. He wanted to become a pianist in Iran until the revolutionary guards raided the block where he lived, heard him practising and threw his music scores out of the window. That and fear of conscription precipitated a decision. He chose to escape.

I consider him as he sits opposite me, thoughtfully stirring more sugar into his black coffee. How would I cope? I can't imagine such trauma and disruption in my young life. I take it for granted that I belong somewhere and have a country that I can always return to after my travels.

As I recall this many years later Khoren's face fades and is replaced by another: the smiling face of a young woman. She is also a pianist, the daughter of a friend I have sadly lost touch with. I did meet her once in Canada when she was only twelve or thirteen years old, already showing promise and rising in the ranks of national competitions for young musicians. Her parents, both part of a diaspora, met and married in their adopted country where she was born and raised. I am full of unease remembering that my friend has not replied to any of my emails since the spectre of Covid began stalking our world. But that is another story which happened much later. I will continue telling this one.

Khoren and I have reached an understanding. He wants to practise his English—and who better to do this with than an English teacher. And I could use a male escort, a sort of protective shield to deflect the local street hounds. So begins our unlikely alliance.

I have concocted a lengthy tourist itinerary to fill my time in Istanbul, and Khoren is happy to tag along. He scales the ramparts of Ottoman castles alongside me, trails willingly around museums of Greco-Roman sculptures and accompanies me into Byzantine churches glittering with mosaics, all the time asking questions: How is this or that word used in English? Do I like Chopin's music? Which country do I like best? I give him an immersion course in Turkish history and culture at the same time, reading aloud from my guidebook as we tick off the sights. He absorbs it all.

One day, we take a break from the agenda and visit Çiçek Pasajı (the Passage of Flowers), not far from the fish market. In a streetside tavern, over some heady draught beer and a plate of fried istavrit (deliciously crispy golden anchovies), we hatch a bizarre plan. Khoren hasn't touched a piano in over eight months, he tells me, looking down at the table. 'Where can we find one?' I ask.

Somehow, he knows that there is one in an auditorium in the British Cultural Centre, a bus ride away. The plan is implausible, but we will go there this afternoon. I will pose as a British talent scout and ask if he can be allowed to play the piano, so that I can assess his skills. I know little about classical music and nothing about playing technique, but at least I won't need to act the British part of our deception, so we convince ourselves that the scheme will work.

The centre is quiet when we arrive, and the Turkish caretaker left in charge has his head on the desk and is taking an afternoon siesta. I give a small cough and he wakes up. He regards me from under heavy eyelids as I make my strange request. With uncharacteristic confidence, I tell him I am British and relate the rest of our invented story, then reach for my passport as proof. I flash it in front of him, hopefully, as I once saw James Bond do to good effect in *The Living Daylights*. Will it gain us entry?

Amazingly, it works. Refusing requires too much effort and he would like to return to his nap, I suspect. Without a word, he rummages in a drawer of the desk and produces a key. He leads us down a passageway and opens the door to the neglected auditorium and leaves us.

Khoren crosses the stage and wipes a film of dust from the piano lid before tentatively raising it. He flexes his fingers a few times and then starts to play while I listen. His plight forgotten for a short while, he becomes absorbed in his playing. At the end

I commend him, although I have no idea if he is an exceptional or a mediocre pianist. We leave, thanking the caretaker, and head back out into the Turkish sunshine.

Two weeks later my time in Istanbul comes to an end and I move on to Mersin—a fourteen-hour bus ride away at the other end of the country, close to the Syrian border, where I am to stay with another Turkish family—hopefully my English lessons will be better received by their children. I say goodbye to Khoren, leaving him to continue the wait for his application to be processed and an onward travel permit issued. We exchange addresses and I promise to stay in touch.

I keep my word.

Some months later when I am back in the UK a postcard arrives. On the front is a picture of one of Istanbul's iconic landmarks, Galata bridge at dusk spanning the Golden Horn with views east towards Asia and west towards Europe. On the back, just two simple words: 'Got it.' I smile to myself. My friend's new life will begin in Canada and once there he will eventually achieve his dream through his daughter, a gifted young musician who plays the piano. This story is for her.

See Greece, Crete, Turkey, Egypt and Israel map on page 243.

Beware of Vipers!

'Be careful! There could be vipers here.' The warning comes from behind me as I brush through the waist-high fronds of bronze bracken. The words whirl inside my head like a small tornado setting off an alarm bell somewhere. Then a sleeping memory stirs, awoken within the quilted folds of my grey matter. It shakes off the accumulated dust of decades and reveals itself. A different time, a different place and another voice, a French one, is issuing the same warning to myself and my best friend Rita: 'Faites attention, il y a des vipéres ici.' We are high in the Alps, in summertime, leaping from stone to stone along a dried-up riverbed.

Rita and I were on the cusp of our adult lives in 1974, even if we were too busy living in the present to think much about what might lie ahead of us. Each morning I woke in this unfamiliar location and, like a child, was enchanted anew by the distant wavering view of ethereal snow-capped peaks from my window. The suburban red-brick homes opposite my parent's house in central England were gone, replaced by this captivating new panorama of the French Alps. It tugged at my eyes like a magnet, until, with a snap, it was broken by the phlegmy coughing of a smoker in the next room. Igor was waking up.

We were here thanks to our French teacher, Mademoiselle Duckworth. She had given us the hotel address to write to. Eighteen and fairly clueless, we were caught in the no-man's land between final school exams and leaving home to start university. So, we listened to her advice and composed a letter to the owner of the family hotel in our best French asking for summer work in the alpine resort of Chamrousse.

We had crossed the channel—or la Manche as we preferred to call it in deference to our French hosts—on the night ferry from Dover to Calais, connecting to Paris, where, bleary-eyed, we changed trains at the Gare de Lyon. From there, with just a baguette and a wheel of camembert to fortify us, we made the long journey down through the middle of France to Grenoble, the self-proclaimed capital of the Alps.

This, we accomplished all by ourselves, without mishap, and despite a very unconfident level of spoken French, taking our first tentative steps into the world beyond the familiar drab concrete teaching blocks of our local comprehensive school.

Equipped with an impressive grasp of French grammar, we could rattle off verb conjugations for multiple verbs in different tenses, like parrots. But we had a vocabulary range which tended towards the literary and fanciful rather than the practical and colloquial language that would have been more useful in France itself. For this, we blamed Balzac, Flaubert and a stack of set texts we had been studying all year. When it came to it, conversing en français proved to be challenging and our comprehension skills also left something to be desired. We were able to speak in

French, but at a pace not much faster than that of an escargot. And we didn't know the French way to say 'um' and 'er' when we needed to fill a thinking pause.

High up in the Alps that day the voice that was issuing the snake warning belonged to the self-assured Jean-Paul. Not much older than us, he was one of two young Frenchmen working at the hotel. Several days previously, we had been introduced to him and his silent companion Jean-Michel. The arrival of the two new waitresses, or serveuses de table—we preferred our more elegant-sounding French job titles—hadn't failed to catch their attention. Rita and I had noticed them too and persuaded ourselves that this afternoon's walk in the mountains was actually a 'date', which might even lend some romantic interest to our stay. But, so far, the two French boys' interest in us appeared more akin to curiosity, or perhaps we just presented a challenge too far. We might just have to settle for a much slower-paced Anglo-French rapprochement.

Jean-Paul, Jean-Michel… Double-barrelled Christian names seemed to grow on French trees here. There was also Jean-Jacques, the hotel propriétaire, and his wife, Marie-Claude, who was in charge of reception. But in the kitchen things were different; this was the territory of staff with single appellations, some of whom were less sympathique towards the two new arrivals from England.

There was our boss, André, in his chef's white jacket, that was a size too small for his stout frame and in danger of pinging its buttons. A nervous chain smoker, he often mysteriously vanished from the kitchen for hours on end. But he was not a problem, since, even when present, he rarely spoke to us.

Unfortunately, his despotic and omnipresent assistant proved more than willing to take over the role of supervising us. This was the thin and choleric François, who we decided was dissatisfied with his life as a mere dishwasher. We never addressed him by his name and referred to him disparagingly behind his back simply as 'le plongeur', his job title, especially when he was being particularly obnoxious.

Like André, he could often be seen attached to a Gauloise cigarette, and he was sometimes entrusted with non-dishwashing tasks, for which he was clearly not suited, at least in our opinion. One day we came across him stirring the contents of a large bubbling vat with an ash-laden cigarette dangling from his lips. Horrified, we watched, realising that those lentils, with their additional carbonized supplements, were destined to become part of the evening meal.

As well as serving at table, our own duties included floor mopping on a daily basis. Standing in the doorway in his white dishwasher's apron and chequered drainpipe trousers, François would regularly inspect the quality of our work.

'C'est sale (it's dirty),' he would remark, running a finger over the floor I had just finished washing.

But François was not our only source of concern in the hotel. Lurking around any corner could be the snake-oiled Igor. To our dismay, we discovered that he also occupied the room next to ours in the basement. A poseur and preener par excellence,

Igor could make a Hyacinth Macaw feel monochrome and scruffy. He would stroll around the hotel joking with the guests and reeking of aftershave. We never really understood what his job was, although he claimed to be manager of the hotel's finance.

'Je suis directeur financier,' he informed us once, stretching out his neck wattles. He played the role of an important friend of the family, but he was one to be avoided by us at all costs. We quickly learned of his close presence either from his heady colognes or from his penchant for cigars. At such times, we turned on our heels or else risked being subjected to wet kisses on both cheeks.

'Ah, c'est la jeune fille anglaise!' he would proclaim if he managed to grab one of us unawares in the kitchen. We learned to accept that we were fair game to this middle-aged Russian with sagging cheek pouches and a wardrobe of garish floral neckerchiefs.

After serving breakfast and doing our cleaning duties, we would take our own breakfast, usually, a bowl of frothy hot chocolate into which we dunked wedges of crusty baguette. Then we had no further duties until dinner time, so we would either join our new friend Brigid, a Swedish yoga instructor, on the roof for a lazy afternoon of sunbathing or an impromptu yoga lesson, or accompany some of the French guests or other members of the hotel staff on a wander through an alpine valley. That day, in the company of Jean-Paul and Jean-Michel, we became unsuspecting prey to the sens de l'humour français. The vipers they claimed were lying in wait caused us to leap out of the dry riverbed in a panic, much to our companions' amusement.

During our month in the Alps, we also found ourselves being initiated into the habits and pastimes of the French en vacances. When we had free time in the evening, we sat around the bar tables with the hotel guests and were instructed in the French passion for playing games. We became skilled players at le trictrac (backgammon) and the popular card game belote, developing a certain fluency in their respective jargons.

On one such evening, wishing to broaden our experience of the finer points of French culture, one guest plied us with glasses of an expensive green liqueur. This was our initiation to Chartreuse, a strong French spirit made according to a secret recipe known only by the Carthusian monks who produced it. The generous owner of the newly purchased bottle impressed upon us that more than 130 different mountain herbs were used in its production. We sipped the fiery liquid obligingly, murmuring, 'C'est bon, c'est très bon,' and making appreciative sounds as the faces of the hotel guests began to swim before our eyes.

Our time in Chamrousse eventually came to an end and, with it, our first real experience of French life and culture. Neither of us had made any progress towards a French romance with either of the Jeans, but our spoken French had definitely improved, and that summer we had taken our first brave steps into an entirely new world.

On the train back to Paris we sat in silence in the restaurant car. On the table stood a half empty bottle of cheap red wine of the kind we were now accustomed to. Our futures lay ahead of us, but in a nostalgic haze, we watched from the window as the mountains of the Alps receded and disappeared from view.

See France map on page 244.

The Reluctant Climber

'**B**ut you are going to climb it, aren't you?' the girl from Singapore asks, regarding me intently as her friend looks on. Sharing the springy back seat of the minibus, my two travelling companions have introduced themselves as we bounce along the road like three synchronized trampoline artists performing in unison.

'Well, I'm not really sure yet,' I prevaricate. 'I thought I might just… um, explore around the base for a while,' I add lamely, avoiding their gaze.

We are in Borneo and boarded the same vehicle several hours earlier in Kota Kinabalu, the coastal capital of Sabah. It's taking us north to the Kinabalu National Park, a large area of pristine rainforest.

At the park's centre towers its majestic namesake, Mount Kinabalu, initially calculated to be 4,101 metres high but later corrected to 4,095 metres. Nevertheless, this is high enough to make it one of the highest peaks in South East Asia, and one which my new acquaintances are going to climb, and I am not.

It is mid-1990 and I haven't been on the island of Borneo long. Hired on a short-term teaching contract at a school in Negara Brunei Darussalam (The sultanate of Brunei), I am in a small country sandwiched between its two larger Malaysian neighbours, Sabah and Sarawak. Finding myself a metaphorical stone's throw from the equator for the first time in my life, I have not yet adapted to the heat and high humidity of the tropics, waking up each morning in a slippery sweat despite the best efforts of an ever-clacking ceiling fan.

One morning, as I lay perspiring on a wrinkled sheet beneath the fan's whirling helicopter blades, an urge came to me to see the beating, green heart of Borneo. But where to go exactly? As I pondered this, an image flashed before my eyes: Marlon Brando's face, framed by luxuriant green vegetation. A film I'd seen—wasn't it set somewhere in Vietnam? In a jungle, with lots of leeches, anyway. It was time to find a place like that and take an exploratory stroll. Borneo must be full of lush leechy rainforest. Later that day at school, I consulted the other expatriate teachers. 'Go to Kinabalu,' one of them advised. 'Lots of leeches there!'

So now the school holidays have finally arrived, and I've come to Sabah in search of a jungle experience. Aside from fulfilment of my fantasy of strolling with leeches, I'm also hoping for something else. Before my departure, I did some preparatory reading and learned that Borneo, the world's third largest island, is an oasis for botanical specialities and the focal point in South East Asia for the carnivorous pitcher plant. Some particularly rare ones are found uniquely on the slopes of Mount Kinabalu.

But, as well as the mountain's herbal carnivores, there are some endemic rhododendrons, flamboyant and larger-than-life specimens. And some exotic little necklace orchids are also on my list to find. There are plenty of interesting plants for an amateur botanist like me.

So, my plan is to spend the next few days stretching my jungle legs on the flat terrain at the foot of the mountain in pursuit of a few botanical prizes. But that was before the minibus journey. I had not reckoned on falling into the clutches of two very assertive and persistent Singaporeans.

By the time we arrive at park headquarters I have almost capitulated. The gist of their argument is that the mountain is there, ipso facto I should climb it, to which I can't think of a good response. Then they mention that climbing it involves an eight-kilometre trek, steep in places, and which does require a bit of advance planning. Doubt floods back. I am totally unprepared for scaling the highest mountain in Borneo. I point this out to the ultra-efficient Singaporeans, but they have done all their homework and the pair of them are a walking-talking textbook of information for anyone needing conversion to the joys of mountaineering. I am not off the hook yet.

'Well, how long will it take?' I ask, still feeling around for excuses and half hoping that eight kilometres up and down might comfortably be completed before lunchtime if I set off promptly after breakfast. I do not get a straight answer.

'It depends how fast you walk. But you can book an overnight stay at the rest house near the top. Then get up early and climb the last part to the summit to see the sun rise. Our guidebook recommends making a two-day hike of it. And, of course, you'll need to buy a climbing permit and hire a guide when we arrive,' the lead girl replies.

I jump in eagerly with another excuse, 'Oh well, I don't know then. I didn't really budget for a guide.'

'No problem,' number two chips in. 'You can share ours. We booked one ahead.'

After that, there isn't much resistance left in me. With a helpful escort on either side, I am gently propelled towards the park reception to register my stay, purchase a climbing permit and make an overnight booking for the rest house near the summit.

We set off early the next morning—there is a knock on my door at 5 a.m. to ensure that I am awake. Twenty minutes later I join them at the start of the trail where they are waiting with their Malaysian guide. As I pause to take stock of how fit and athletic they look, and note their new climbing boots and trekking poles, my stomach begins to churn like a washing machine. I'm not sure if it is nerves or because I've had to skip breakfast.

But there's no time to mess about. With their guide leading the way, my mentors stride off and I fall in behind. We enter the forest. It's my first immersion in real jungle and my untuned ears are surprised to register the soundscape. Accompanying us as we walk, there is a backdrop of continual buzzing interrupted from time to time by an excited screech. Somewhere nearby but hidden from view there seems to be a party going on, and the vociferous guests are birds and insects, none of which I can actually see.

This first part of the trail is montane oak forest, and the trees are rather different from the English oaks I am familiar with. These are giant tropical oaks that are recognisable from their acorns the size of golf balls. I notice that the path is ascending slowly. Good, I think, somewhat optimistically; I am still hoping that it will turn out to be a gentle stroll.

But as the morning progresses, the heat mounts and the park headquarters are left far behind. We climb into dense jungle, which starts to crowd in uncomfortably close. I pick my way carefully along the narrow trail between watching walls of thick green vegetation on either side. It's a chaotic tangle of growth, armed with hooks and claws that reach out to grab me as I pass. I'm also on the lookout for leeches. One of the expat teachers said they wave their thin black bodies at you from the leaves as you pass, not exactly in friendly greeting but more in a 'what's for lunch?' style of enquiry. I tentatively expose my arm as bait, but there are no takers, so I walk on.

Pausing to wipe away the beadlets of sweat on my brow, I try to visually untangle the world around me. My eyes are adjusting to the different kinds of vegetation now. Here and there I can even distinguish individual plant parts. Tropical leaves are not uniformly green. Some are white, orange or red, surprisingly waxy to the touch and tapering into elongated tips. These are the drip-tips I have read about: an evolutionary adaptation, by allowing the rainwater to run off faster they speed up drying and prevent the loss of nutrients. And the variation in colour signifies the presence of different pigments, which protect the young leaves from the harsh tropical sun. I look up to share this information with the Singaporeans, but it's too late; they have marched ahead.

The path curves and I wonder what lurks around the next bend. It's an ever-changing canvas and I'm half-expecting to meet the coal-black eyes of Rousseau's crouching tiger, shortly. I hurry on finding no tigers but splashes of crimson on the soil, instead—not blood from a leech-fest victim but creeping ground figs, a different kind to the only ones I know that come dried in a rectangular box with rounded ends in the Christmas season.

There's another species of tropical fig here that I've seen in natural history documentaries on television: the parasitic strangler fig. Its seeds grow from a bird dropping on a tree branch. They encase their host in a living tomb as they climb higher to reach the light in the canopy. A ripple of movement makes me look up, but it is only the muscular calves of my adrenaline-charged companions disappearing up ahead. Their pace is challenging. I hesitate and wonder if it's not too late to turn back. No. I'm committed now. I have to catch up with them.

I walk then stop again. Something else from my 'must-see' list. Suspended from a wiry tendril is a dangling carnivore. I have just seen my first pitcher plant. I inspect its modified leaves that have become hanging death traps, pitcher receptacles into which the plant pours digestive juices.

The hairy-lidded specimen in front of me is one of at least sixteen species present on Mount Kinabalu; the largest, apparently, has pitchers with stomachs that can hold several litres of liquid. This is sufficient to drown and digest any small unwary mammal, insect or bird that has been lured by pheromones and has slipped into the enzymatic soup below. I peer inside the biggest pitcher, anticipating blood and gore, but there are only a few insect legs floating languidly on the surface. Not much goes to waste here. With such fascinating distractions, I am losing my fear and beginning to enjoy this chamber of tropical horrors.

Unfortunately, I have fallen far behind the Singaporeans and their guide who are no longer in sight. When I eventually stumble, out of breath, into the first of the marked trail shelters at 1981 metres, I find them waiting, rested, and feeding a queue of tame ground squirrels with snack leftovers. They are ready to move on and stand up, but then hesitate, looking uncomfortable. I speak first. 'I think I'm holding you up. Perhaps it's better if you don't wait for me.' There is a short silence. Having been a little overhasty in taking a novice mountain climber into their charge, they are now reluctant to abandon me. They protest, but not too much. I reassure them, 'I'll be fine, don't worry. We can meet up at the lodge later, can't we?'

It's agreed and I promise faithfully not to venture off the path—although secretly I decide I will if I see something really interesting. With relief, we part company. Now I'm alone and can take my time.

The trail has become steeper at this altitude, and the knotted roots of trees, spread out across the thin topsoil seeking an anchor point and forming a series of uneven 'steps', are intent on tripping careless feet. Quite suddenly, the first mountain rhododendrons appear. Stiff, leafy neck ruffs encase stunning heads of canary-yellow or apricot-orange flowers. Like first prize exhibits in a horticultural show, they seem out of place here and are a surreal vision on the mountainside.

At 2000 metres the vegetation dramatically changes. It is sparser here and the trees are stunted. I must have reached the cloud forest, not far below the treeline now. Stooping, twisted trunks of dwarf trees are draped in mossy blankets that support a community of epiphytes, plants with roots not in soil but air, while they tenaciously cling onto the green velvet branches of their hosts. The moss supports a platoon of pink-helmeted soldier lichen too, parading through toy town. The forest has taken on an elfin guise.

My breathing has become more laboured in the thin air, and as I pause to take in the miniature landscape around me, I realise that my feet are hurting—Oh, no! Blisters are the last thing I need! Another sign that I should have stayed down at the mountain base. But it's too late for regrets. I press on and cross the tree line. Most plant life is unable to grow at this altitude and soon there is no obvious path, only exposed rock for me to clamber over, tired and panting.

Finally, the Laban Rata Resthouse comes into view, perched on a granite outcrop. Despite being in the tropics, it's cooler up here. Inside the lodge another climber is sitting with his head in his hands and complaining of a headache. He looks up as I enter. Blank eyes in a white face. Altitude sickness.

On a balcony, overlooking the rocky vista, I find the Singaporean girls, apparently, unaffected and relaxing with hot coffee. They are already unpacking extra jackets, hats and gloves they have prudently brought with them for tomorrow's pre-dawn ascent on the summit. Seeing me, they look slightly surprised. Did they think I'd get lost? Then one of them reaches into her pack and pulls out a spare pair of leggings. Wordlessly, she hands them to me.

At 3 a.m. everyone is woken for the final push to the top. We climb in darkness and in silence. The only sound is our breathing, shallow and noisy, as we struggle, sometimes on all fours, up the sheer bare rock.

The near-freezing temperature penetrates to our bones. Surprising us, the outline of the top appears, suddenly, like a shrouded black ghost emerging out of the night sky. We are at the summit. In the chilled air, we hunker down and wait for the dawn.

It comes, unremarkable at first. A faint glimmer in the dark sky that expands into fine slivers of delicate pale light reaching out across the far horizon. They coalesce and the colour deepens to form a glowing band of gold that slowly lifts the veil. An undulating blanket is exposed in the valley far beneath us. The waking jungle canopy stretches out towards the ends of the earth.

The sun, now a rising yellow hump, pushes ever upwards, and the sky becomes suffused with intense blue. More light and warmth are cast over the vast rainforest, which responds by sending downy white clouds up to greet the morning. Within a short time, they close together, drawing the veil back over the view. The spectacular show is over.

Together, we start our long and stumbling descent. My head is crowded with impressions jostling for attention. Even if it was hard, it was well worth it. The climb up provided a kaleidoscope of botanical revelations, and then that amazing view of the world at the summit! How would I remember it all? I notice the Singaporeans have stopped on the track ahead and are waiting for me. They have been quietly talking together. Now they are looking at me intently again. For a moment, I am afraid they are going to suggest another mountain that needs climbing somewhere else. But it is not that.

'You know,' one of them announces as she falls in step beside me. 'You surprised us. In the minibus coming here, we thought you weren't going to climb it.'

See Borneo and East Malaysia map on page 242.

Seeing Red in the Canary Islands

Treading carefully to avoid slipping, I follow the zigzag path down the steep hillside of Barranco de Guiniguada into the ravine of the botanic garden of Gran Canaria. It's late September. Most plants have finished flowering and look tired and scruffy. Their rejuvenation in the springtime is still a long way off.

No flowers then, but I pause to admire the palms, which come in all shapes and sizes here, including the bodybuilder of all palms—the mister muscle-bound, endemic Dragon Tree. In one grove, several specimens of this tree stand erect, displaying a ring of sausage-shaped branches which support the palm's dense green canopy.

Further along the path, I arrive at a bridge straddling a gorge, where a sign informs me that the giant Gran Canarian lizard is also present. I lean over and spy one, peeping out from a rocky crevice. It's a dark monster, prehistoric-looking but, fortunately, vegetarian. Another one is splayed out on the rock face. It's a sheer drop down into the gorge, but the lizard looks relaxed, defying gravity with claws that grip like superglue.

I walk on, my interest aroused. I sense that another discovery is imminent. It comes in a dry grove of prickly pear cactus. Some are strangely white and a transfixing sight: an ethereal Christmas scene of seemingly snow-clad cacti.

Prickly pear cacti were brought to southern Europe and the Canary islands from their native habitat in the Americas and cultivated for their edible tunera (pears). Here they stand with their flat lateral stems stretching awkwardly outwards. Resembling fleshy lobes, they are studded with protective spines—the reduced 'leaves' of the cactus.

I move closer, trying to avoid the lethal spines, so that I can examine the white stuff decorating them. An early frost, perhaps? I insert my fingers and take a pinch. No, it's a mysterious white powder and something else. It contains some tiny oval bugs. Squashed with my thumb they spurt a vibrant red slash of colour: bright vermillion 'blood'.

A vague memory of something I have read about the Canary Isles surfaces in my brain and the mystery is solved: coccineal— the source of carmine dye since ancient times. These are female coccineal bugs. Living in colonies while feeding on cactus sap, they secrete waxy snow-white fibres to protect themselves from the sun's heat.

Europeans crossing to the Americas first learned from the Aztecs about using cochineal as a dye for cloth and an important trade began. In their home region, the bugs are still cultivated in prickly pear plantations. In Peru they are harvested, dried and still used as food dye in sweets and confectionery, and colourant in cosmetic products including lipstick and eye shadow. But to produce even a small quantity of dye, tens of thousands of dried insects need to be boiled so that their bodies release carminic acid, which is then mixed with chemicals to give the dye its long-lasting quality.

On Gran Canaria coccineal production has all but disappeared with the rise of synthetic dyes, but in the 1800s, not far from here, the town of Arucas grew prosperous from coccineal. Now only a few local artisans continue collecting the bugs to dye their knitting yarn and fabric naturally.

After that first time in the botanic garden, I encounter the coccineal bug often, on wasteland and roadsides across Gran Canaria. Wherever the prickly pear cactus colonises, the insect follows its food plant. And seeing them again, the memory of that first vermillion streak on my fingers returns.

See Spain and Canary Islands map on page 238.

Food for Thought

Mix-Mix to Go

'The cook is sick,' announces Gedé, first-born son of my Indonesian host family. Unsure how to react, I nod and try to look concerned. Why is he telling me this? Will we go hungry? Or does he want me to cook the evening meal? Neither, I hope.

I am on Lombok island, named after its formidable chilli pepper. And I'm occupying the best room in the house, which has been vacated by Gedé for me, the guest English teacher. The room faces onto a central courtyard with a red earth floor, which bakes harder each day under a blue cloudless sky.

A dusty banana palm, with torn flapping leaves, stands in one corner of the courtyard, with a table and some hot plastic chairs scattered beneath it. The table is the focal point for meals. The family are descended from Balinese Hindus from the neighbouring island, and, taking pride of place on the upper floor of their home, there is also a small traditional altar for daily worship and offerings of food and flowers.

Food is a daily ritual. Every day I share in the family meals, starting with breakfast—an eye-catching palette of local fruit. Today: mango, starfruit, pisang kecil (small bananas) and purple ping-pong balls with transparent viscous centres with the unappetising name of mata kucing (cat's eyes) but delicious in spite of that. Beside the fruit there is always a small pile of salt to replace that lost through perspiration in the ninety percent humidity this part of the world experiences.

But it's the evening meal that I most look forward to. The hired cook from the village works over a single flame in the corner of the courtyard with a wok and an array of unfamiliar fresh herbs and exotic spices, producing culinary masterpieces with exquisite flavours and equally delectable names. Yesterday it was pecel lele (fried catfish) with sambal, a fiery sauce—simultaneously sweet, sour and spicy—accompanied by sop kaki kambing (goat leg soup). And this evening?

This evening I have noticed that something is wrong. There is no tantalising aroma of marinated fish or chicken wafting out from the kitchen in the corner; no sizzling sounds as more ingredients are thrown in and pan-tossed. As mealtime approaches, my stomach begins to rumble its concern, but there is no sign of any cooking activity.

Gedé is still looking at me expectantly for my response when second son Madé wobbles in. He is half-hidden behind the unsteady stack of banana leaves he carries. I watch from the doorway of my room as he tips them unceremoniously onto the communal table. What is going on? The banana leaves are folded together to form small green cubes. Containers of some sort. Then it dawns on me and I shout a silent hurrah. We won't starve and I don't have to cook! Takeaway supper for seven has arrived.

Each folded banana leaf is pinned securely together with bamboo splinters. Opened, it reveals either an individual portion of steaming coconut rice, or one of the main dish, gado-gado, so-called 'mix-mix'. Its name is a perfect description of its contents: crunchy local vegetables and chopped hard-boiled egg, topped with krupuk (prawn crackers) smothered in a delicious peanut sauce. Madé has brought our evening meal from a warung, a roadside food stall. With banana leaves and bamboo pins, this Indonesian speciality has been wrapped Lombok-style to go. Here, nature provides simple sustainable solutions for everyday needs.

Other family members appear from all directions; plastic chairs are pulled up, and we arrange ourselves around the small table. 'Selamat makan (Enjoy your meal),' we bid each other politely as we unpin our portions. Then a silence descends as seven backs bend over their leafy plates to eat.

See Indonesia map on page 246.

A Taste of French Cake

Exhumed today, from deep inside a cylindrical cardboard tube—a piece of my past has dropped out. Scrabbling around up in my loft, I was searching for something else but have found 1976 instead. A time long past has come to light with the help of three wall posters.

The first poster looks like an abstract painting by Mondrian: twelve criss-crossing lines, angular and erratic, with dots of colour along their lengths. This poster shows the Paris Métro network with all its stations. The next is a black and white photo poster of the river Seine in wintertime, its flowing water stroked by snow-laden tree branches. The third is a print portrait of a frail, pasty-faced young man in a dark suit and cravat with a white orchid in his lapel. My year of living in the French capital is laid bare in a roll of crumpled posters.

I unfurl the Métro plan and place an index finger on the river Seine, a pale blue horizontal band that bisects the middle of it. My eyes rove outwards seeking something but not finding it, so I slide my finger up and over the blue band to the Right Bank and then slightly to the right. There! Line 5. Marked in orange. I trace it upwards from station to station, jumping between République and Gare de L'Est. Then on again to Jaurès. Names that are strangely familiar, although it is many years since I have travelled this Métro line.

Next stop and I've found what I'm looking for. My finger is right on it now: Métro Laumière. A short walk from Rue Meynadier. The street where I lived in a tiny studio apartment on the top floor. Home for a year, with no lift and 105 steps to climb. Not a problem for the younger me. On the landing outside was a shared toilet—an old-fashioned one, the squat variety. And with an unreliable lock on the door.

On the positive side, my one room apartment had a so-called false balcony, or balconette, a railing that ran around the outside of the floor-length window. Opening over the rooftops of Paris, it offered a wonderful view. And it was a perfect balcony from which a Juliet might ruminate about her Romeo, although its fifth-floor location deterred all the potential French Romeos of my acquaintance.

Less romantically, it faced towards the Gare de l'Est, from which the rhythmic rumble of passing goods trains would reach out to wake me in the silence of the night. When I couldn't get back to sleep I would listen to a cassette tape, usually Bob Dylan's 'Blood on the Tracks', a favourite album at the time, and one which seemed oddly appropriate.

I lift my finger from Laumière and put it down again in a different place; the end of the blue line. I'm looking for another station on Line 1 this time. Here it is: Porte de Vincennes, the Métro stop for the lycée where I was spending my year working as an Assistante d'Anglais (English language assistant), not yet a fully-fledged teacher—that came a few years later. I let the map spring back into a tight roll and push it aside so that I can examine the second poster.

The Seine in wintry monochrome. It's a view of the Left Bank and I can make out the grey line of book stalls on this side of the river, where the bouquinistes ply their trade even in the coldest season. Here bibliophiles browse displays of second-hand books and their titles, all displayed in neat lines, like overlaid cards in a game of solitaire. From pegs above hang imprints and collectable magazines, faded and yellowing, resembling a row of drying handkerchiefs.

I often lingered at these stalls not looking for anything in particular but captivated by the satirical French cartoons, which I did not understand, and by the beautiful marbled endpapers of the antiquarian books. Not far from here, I remember, was a bookstore, Shakespeare and Company, successor to the iconic English-language bookshop founded by Sylvia Beach. In her time, Miss Beach was friend and benefactor to many of the French, American and British literati living in Paris in the early decades of the 1900s: James Joyce, André Gide, Ernest Hemingway, T.S. Eliot, Ezra Pound and other 'Greats' whose works I was studying on my university course. I was in awe of all of them.

Once, while perusing the books on the shelves of Shakespeare and Company, I was invited to join other browsers for a coffee and a chat about books upstairs. I thought little of it at the time, and, although I remember climbing the creaky backstairs leading up to a small room, I recall nothing of the coffee or the rarefied conversation that undoubtedly took place.

Some while afterwards, I heard that such invitations were a privilege accorded to only a select few of the bookstore visitors, those who somehow caught the current owner's eye by looking sufficiently 'interesting'. I wonder what it was about me, a 21-year-old student, that could possibly have secured me that invitation?

I release the poster edges and watch as two rolling tidal waves clash back together over the waters of the Seine. Then I move it aside and consider the final poster: the one of the sickly-looking young man in a black suit. His dark hair lies flat against his scalp and is scrupulously parted down the centre. Above his upper lip sprout the youthful fine hairs of a moustache that he is trying to grow, perhaps to appear older. The eyes are his most striking feature: dark, wide, deep-set, almost hypnotic. It's a portrait, painted in 1892. I gaze at his face and remember.

It was nearing the end of my year in France and a long week-end, one extending into three days by the bridge of a national holiday—what the French aptly called 'un pont'. I had taken the train heading south-west out of Paris to the city of Chartres, where I stayed overnight. The next morning I boarded a local bus, which meandered through the French countryside before eventually setting me down in the small town of Illiers, now called Illiers-Combray. In a strange case of real life imitating fiction, it had been renamed just five years previously.[1]

---

1   *Combray was the fictitious name that Proust gave to the town where he spent his childhood holidays in his aunt's home. Illiers was renamed*

Midday was approaching when I crossed the town's small central square, but everything was quiet. I had been looking for a clue as to where the house might lie. In a side street, I found it, quite by chance—a small cottage with a garden and a pebbled path leading up to the front door, half-concealed by an overhanging branch of flowering wisteria.

My knocking produced no response, at first. Then an old man, in baggy blue work trousers and a knitted waistcoat, appeared behind me. He was the caretaker.

'Oui Mademoiselle. C'est la maison de Tante Léonie,' he confirmed, and taking a key from his waistcoat pocket, he unlocked the door to Aunt Léonie's house and led me inside.

That day I was the only visitor to the house, made famous not on account of the owner herself but because of her relationship to the young man on my poster. He was her nephew, the French novelist Marcel Proust, and it was at his aunt's provincial home that the writer had spent his childhood holidays, and which now also served as a museum of Proustian memorabilia.

All seven volumes of Proust's literary masterpiece *In Search of Lost Time* were set reading on my university course, but at the time of my visit, I was still only halfway through volume three. Since I was having to reading *À la Recherche du Temps Perdu* in French, I was also painfully focused on grasping the semantic meanings of the impossibly long sentences I was struggling to disentangle. Nevertheless, I was fascinated by the author and

Illiers-Combray by its inhabitants in the early 1970s in honour of their most famous summer resident.

his semi-autobiographical work, which painted a picture of life within the aristocratic social circles and artistic salons of France at the end of the nineteenth century.

The concierge led me through the living room and up the stairs to the small bedroom that the young Marcel occupied during his stays there. The walls, bedecked in ageing flowery wallpaper, crowded in on us as we stood surveying Marcel's small wooden bed. Then my eyes were drawn to the table beside it and to a metal contraption with a ceramic base that resembled a submarine periscope. Some faded picture slides lay nearby.

'Ça, Mademoiselle, c'est la lanterne magique,' my guide announced.

The real one? The magic lantern described in the opening chapter of volume one of Proust's work? Yes, the same. It was an early form of slide projector, used by the boy Marcel to project picture stories onto his bedroom wall as he pined for his absent mother. The physical reality of the lantern in front of me came as a shock. So, it was true. Somehow, the effort of deciphering those multi-claused sentences on the printed page had prevented me from appreciating the autobiographical detail of the story, even if I had believed in it enough to make my own literary pilgrimage here.

Strangely overwhelmed by this revelation, I don't remember the rest of the house tour except the end. I was making my way out though the small French kitchen when I noticed a plate of petites madeleines on the table, small shell-shaped sponge cakes that had been intentionally put on display to remind the visitor of another key incident in the Proustian epic. The moment when the adult Marcel dips a crumbling madeleine cake into a lime flower tisane and tastes it. The effect is to transport him back through the years, unlocking a flood of unexpected memories in the process.

Dormant memories. My own have been awakened after some forty years. I raise my hands and the literary hero of my year in France snaps out of sight as the poster flips back into a tight roll. Bundling all three posters together, I return them to the cardboard tube locking up 1976 until my next visit to the loft. I give a wry smile and my madeleine moment is over.

See France map on page 244.

Lessons in English
for Gastronomic Purposes

'**B**e careful not to roll off the edge.' These were the parting words of Johan, owner of Gili Guesthouse, as he descended the ladder to the beach fifteen feet below. I was left on the rickety platform. Perching on a bamboo frame, it had presumably been built as a lookout post for a beach lifeguard who was habitually never present. This was my temporary bedroom for the night, as I had reluctantly surrendered my own to two members of a Dutch tour group. They would sleep inside my beach chalet under my mosquito net, while I would have to make do with the thin mattress that Johan had helped me drag up the ladder to my new high-rise sleeping quarters. I raised my eyes to the night sky in search of help. My mosquito net would be useless on this bare platform anyway. There was nowhere to secure it unless I could lasso one or two of those twinkling stars in the Southern Cross. After positioning the mattress as far away from the edge as possible, I cocooned myself in a sarong and lay down with the consoling thought that perhaps mosquitoes couldn't fly up to this altitude.

It was 1988 and I was travelling through the Indonesian archipelago with a stop here and there to pay for my board and lodgings as an English tutor. On the island of Java I spent a month in the steamy sprawling suburbs of the capital, a forty-minute bone-shaking ride from the central bus station in Jakarta where people swarmed about like bees in a hive. Staying with family number one on the city outskirts, I sometimes managed to cadge a lift downtown in the chauffeur-driven limousine which carried the father to his company office each day. It was deliciously air-conditioned and pure bliss to stretch back on its white leather back seat and enjoy a brief escape from the saturating tropical heat.

Unused to the high humidity, I had struggled to sleep at the beginning of my stay. I lay spreadeagled like a heat-stressed starfish beside what I took to be a giant toothpaste tube, occupying a substantial part of the narrow bed. It was, I decided, a pillow of sorts although a very solid one. I tried stuffing a section of it under my head with the remainder hanging off the side of the bed, but this only served to give me neckache. In a frustrated sweat, I pushed the offending object off the bed onto the floor.

I questioned my host family about its purpose the next day. 'Something for hugging in the night,' they explained, 'it's called a "Dutch wife".' I nodded, although none the wiser. I later learned that these rock-hard bedroom bolsters, a common feature in Indonesian bedrooms, had been of great comfort to homesick Dutch soldiers during the colonial period. From that day on, wherever I found one in my sleeping quarters I dispatched it immediately to the floor.

The 'Dutch wife' was not the only colonial legacy I encountered in twentieth century Indonesia. From time to time, I heard Dutch loanwords spoken in Indonesian and found an occasional Dutch influence in Indonesian cuisine. So, the sight of a small, overloaded boat disgorging its cargo of excited Dutch tourists onto the fine white sand that afternoon on Gili island was not entirely a surprise. But in order to explain how we all came to be on a remote coral atoll, I should first backtrack a little.

After a month in Jakarta, I continued my journey and travelled eastwards across Java towards the location for my second tutoring assignment. It was a circuitous route that took in ancient temples, batik workshops and occasional stops for hikes up active volcanoes. Eventually I arrived on Lombok, the next Indonesian island along after Bali. There, a family of five Balinese Hindus welcomed me into their modest family home in Mataram, the provincial capital. I was to stay a month with them and help their eldest son improve his English.

But my stay was unexpectedly cut short. After just a few days, my tutee announced a change of plan. 'Now please you go Gili Meno for learn cook English.'

I was rather confused, especially as I had only set eyes on him twice since my arrival, due to his mysterious disappearances for long periods without explanation. Had I failed to live up to expectation? But, as I discovered, with some relief, there was no threat to my professional reputation. Family number two did not actually want to get rid of me. An unexpected problem had arisen.

A cousin had fallen ill and was in hospital. Patients in Indonesian hospitals need to be cared for principally by their relatives while they waited for a visit from the doctor to prescribe their treatment. The wait was taking some time as such visits were an occurrence almost as rare as a sighting of the critically endangered Balinese starling. My tutee was spending nearly all his time at the hospital delivering clean laundry, meals and medication to his ailing cousin. There was no time in his busy schedule for English lessons.

Up to this point, I had been hanging around the house in Mataram, in case my tutee showed up for a lesson. My days passed in the company of other family members in the forecourt of their home, where we sat under a huge tree whose spreading branches provided ample shade from the strong sun. There, we communed with visitors and passers-by, and, in this way, I got to know the neighbourhood quite well in a short time.

On one afternoon, an old woman with a bundle of wares to sell squatted down on the doorstep to pause on her rounds. Grinning broadly, she displayed an uneven set of red-stained teeth as she took a small cloth package from her sleeve and unwrapped it. With the aid of some sign language and a pocket Indonesian dictionary, I learned that it contained areca nut, lime and some squares of betel leaf. She wrapped the nut and lime in a leaf to make a small wad then popped it into her mouth and began chewing. Seeing my interest in this local recreational stimulant, she offered me some. I declined, fearing that my 'Boots the Chemists' travel toothpaste would not be up to the task of removing red betelnut stains.

With my tutee absent, redundancy was now on the cards, so I accepted the alternative offered to me. As far as I could understand, this would be with an island-dwelling cook in a location I was yet to find. I followed the family's instructions and travelled to a small coastal village from where boats sometimes left for Gili Meno. Gili Meno, or middle island, was unsurprisingly the middle atoll in a trio known as the Gili islands, which lay off the northwest coast of Lombok. There, at a beachside guesthouse for backpackers, my mission was to tutor a cook in the much-neglected specialism of English for gastronomic purposes. It was not my particular area of expertise, but I was willing to give it a go.

Teaching the resident cook at Gili Guesthouse turned out not to be a straightforward matter. Johan, the guesthouse owner, was of Dutch-Indonesian descent and spoke English, his third language, very well, but Kersen, the cook, whose name meant 'cherry' in English, spoke only Indonesian, and Johan was keen that he should at least be able to communicate about meals with the backpacker guests.

For our first lesson, I decided to plunge straight in with some simple naming of culinary essentials in my student's workplace, the kitchen. Cherry was busy preparing freshly caught fish for lunch when I entered. A pan of water was on the stove ready to receive rice from a nearby sack. Rice was an easy and useful word to start with. A bonus was that I knew the word in Indonesian too as nasi goreng (fried rice), which had been one of my regular mealtime choices from menus across the Indonesian archipelago.

I pointed to the rice and confidently pronounced its name in Indonesian and then in English, 'Nasi…rice.'

'Bukan nasi (not rice). Beras,' corrected Cherry, without looking up from his fish chopping.

I hurriedly consulted my pocket dictionary and discovered my mistake. In Indonesian, it appeared that only cooked rice was nasi. Uncooked rice was beras. How to explain that English only had one word for rice, whatever its state? Was this going to turn into a how-many-words-do-Eskimos-have-for-snow kind of conundrum?

I moved the lesson swiftly on, pointing to the fish lying inert on the chopping board as it waited for the fall of Cherry's knife. 'Ikan,' I said. Then slightly less confidently, 'fish.' Cherry remained silent. I felt reassured and continued, pointing to another fish and repeated 'Ikan…fish.' Cherry paused his knife. This, it seemed, was not enough. With a dismissive wave of his knife, he proceeded to point to each unrecognisable marine specimen, lined up awaiting its turn on the board, and then named it in Indonesian. I was out of my depth. I could barely tell a trout from a goldfish. And I was no marine biologist. Mortified, I adjourned the lesson until the following day and went down to the beach to rethink my lesson plan.

Johan laughed when I told him about it later but encouraged me to continue. He seemed satisfied when, after a few days of coaching, the punctilious Cherry was able to greet guests at mealtimes with a cheery 'Good morning', 'Good afternoon' or 'Good evening', as appropriate. We were making steady progress with a few safe non-gastronomic essentials.

And then the Dutch arrived, shattering the serenity of the beach as they tumbled ashore, where I lay quietly mulling over my lesson plans. A couple of backpackers lounging nearby looked up from their game of backgammon, beneath the shady fronds of a coconut palm. The day-tripping Dutch had come seeking the novelty of a coral island and to frolic in the aquamarine water, snorkel among the fishes and eat whatever was on offer, which I noted that lunchtime was ikan bakar: grilled fish, species unknown. However, they got slightly more than they bargained for. After a day of fun and frolicking, they were ready to return to their comfortable hotel on Lombok and enquired of Johan when the boat would come. A rapid conversation ensued in Dutch. The last public boat had left hours ago, Johan explained. If they hadn't booked a boat to return—and they hadn't—they were stuck here for the night. Being part Dutch, Johan felt compelled to make a gesture of kinship and offered to accommodate them in the chalets of Gili Guesthouse. This was how I came to be spending the night on a lifeguard's lookout platform with the waves gently lapping beneath me.

I woke in the morning to the sound of splashing. Some of the Dutch were taking a pre-breakfast dip below me. Peering over the edge of my sleeping platform, which by some miracle I hadn't rolled off, I could see Cherry preparing a mountain of unfamiliar fruit to feed the hungry group before their departure.

The lesson that day would have to be on the naming of fruit then. I felt sure I could count on Cherry to instruct me on their names in Indonesian. I just hoped that my pocket dictionary would be up to the task of translating them.

See Indonesia map on page 246.

Gelato—As It Once Was

'Scusi c'è una gelateria qui vicino?' I enquire at the hotel front desk. It's the last evening of my return visit to Milan and I still haven't enjoyed the pleasure of Italian ice cream. With a knowing smile, the receptionist points in the direction of the nearby square. 'Si Signora, nella piazza a destra. Si chiama Grom.'

It's called Grom? I must look sceptical, but I suspend my disbelief and thank him. Privately, I doubt that a gelateria sounding like a road haulage company will serve good ice cream.

Stepping out of the air-conditioned lobby is like immersing myself in a warm bath. Siesta time is over; the city is coming back to life. And the shops have re-opened. Sylphlike young women are already strolling out, talking animatedly on their mobile phones, Armani and Gucci carrier bags swinging from slim wrists and carefully manicured hands. Fashion shopping isn't on my itinerary any longer—my own 'sylphlike' figure abandoned me a while ago—but it's nice to see that it's still taken seriously here in Milan.

I turn right at the corner, *a destra* as instructed, and need to skirt the edge of a sea of outdoor café tables spilling in all directions across the pavement. Most are occupied by youthful

Milanese, wholesome and healthy-looking, sitting with one of their five a day in front of them. No water bottles are in sight. Is drinking fruit juice a new trend, I wonder? Peach, orange, pineapple and pear are casually scattered across the table tops, their colours reproduce the happy mood of a Miró composition, but I notice a Peroni beer and the illusion is broken.

That essential fashion accessory for any self-respecting millennial, the mobile phone, is everywhere, lying in readiness or held in use. One, in the hand of a young man who has stepped out of a Caravaggio painting, starts to tinkle its theme tune. A tee shirt sculpts his well-toned torso and my eyes are momentarily held. 'Ciao Bello,' I murmur to myself, while enjoying the fleeting image of taking an aperitivo with a toyboy.

I move on and a waft of warm air stirs the café awning as I pass under it. Since I arrived, I've been wondering if I will find Milan changed. It's been twenty years since my last trip here. A part of the older and more worldly-wise me is prepared for disappointment. I remember some cautionary advice about return visits: if you go to a place twice, each time it's a different story. But the world is a finite place and revisiting a haunt of the past seems to happen to me more often as the years go by.

I reach the square and there is Gelateria Grom, proudly displaying its claim to offer 'il gelato come una volta': Ice cream as it once was. The promise fills me with hope, but I'm surprised to find a line of people standing outside the small ice cream kiosk. A queue? Since when has queuing been part of Italian culture? Secretly, I'm reassured. Ice cream that you need to wait for must be worth it.

I survey the scene: a gaggle of laughing school friends; an oblivious couple enjoying a romantic moment; parents with bambini in state-of-the-art buggies. It's a cross-section of Milanese society, all hungry for gelato. I add myself behind the last in the line and study the ice cream board.

The list is impressively long and a masterpiece of inventiveness. My eyes flit between the 'classici' and 'speciali', trying to take them all in. Some of the specialities induce thrills of mouth-tingling anticipation—chestnut, ricotta and fig, cassata, one with extract of liquorice, and the wildly exotic flavour of the month: cream of saffron. Am I feeling bold enough to experiment today?

The quickened tempo of rising voices in the queue ahead distracts me from my decision making. A passionate argument breaks out. Someone is trying to push in and has been noticed. Orderly line formation is proving to be a challenging concept.

Despite the general air of conviviality, everyone has been keeping a sharp eye out for wily queue jumpers. These are streetwise Italians, after all. My ears start to attune to the rising voices and that familiar underlying melodious sound as they engage in lively exchanges of opinion again. It takes me back and is strangely comforting. After a moment the eruption subsides, pitches descend and voices settle back into a steady conversational rhythm. The ice cream queue radiates confident expectation once more.

Little by little, our unruly line is being swallowed into the mouth of the kiosk. We ripple forward like a caterpillar, each segment holding its place. From the exit people are appearing, loaded with full tubs and towering cones. My turn is fast approaching. Hopefully, Grom will not disappoint.

The woman in front has placed a large order. I am grateful and use the opportunity to review the list for one last time. Then I'm at the counter, squashed up against the glass and feeling like a pressed flower.

'Prego Signora?' Help! I hesitate for a fatal moment and miss out on the flavour-of-the-month experience, instead ordering a safe double classic—pistacchio and cioccolato, and just 'un cono piccolo, per favore.' Fear has held me back.

Then, with Olympic gelato held high, I emerge, feeling mildly victorious. Outside, there is a small space on a nearby bench, between a mobile owner and a fellow cone carrier. I squeeze myself into it.

My ice cream is already protesting about the heat and escaping in drips. Time to act. I raise the cone. My tongue reaches out. I close my eyes and smile—gelato as it once was. There are some things, thankfully, which haven't changed.

See Italy map on page 240.

Table Manners for Eating Noodles

S ummoning up my courage, I walked into the ramen-ya. I was a newly arrived foreigner, a gaijin, in a brightly lit noodle shop in a small Japanese town, and I wouldn't go unnoticed. But I was hungry and wanted to try the house speciality.

On the menu board outside, the large knot of brown noodles floating in a soupy sea looked appetising enough. I had read that ramen had been eaten since ancient Edo times and were so popular they could claim to be Japan's national dish. I was keen to try them.

After studying the picture carefully, I tentatively placed my order, persuaded by the slivers of pork and nori seaweed in amongst the noodles, and cubes of white tofu and chopped scallions floating on the surface.

I sat down at a table and waited for my order. Feeling nervous, I glanced quickly around the restaurant. The only other customers were a Japanese family of four, too busy eating to pay the gaijin much attention. I relaxed.

In front of me lay a small paper envelope from which a pair of waribashi protruded—throwaway bamboo chopsticks, split halfway and ready for use. I knew about them from my book on

Japanese etiquette. I fingered them lightly, resisting the desire to pull them apart immediately.

The waiter arrived with my noodles. 'Douzo,' he said, and with a slight bow he placed a steaming bowl before me. I waited for him to leave then snapped the chopsticks apart. A clean break—good. I dipped them into the noodle knot, exploring, and taking care not to spear. Concentrating like a surgeon, I teased a loose noodle strand from the slippery mass. I clasped it firmly and raised it to my mouth, remembering to suck gently without slurping too much. So far so good.

Hearing a sound, my chopsticks trembled in my hand. I froze, momentarily, over my noodle bowl and raised my head. On the neighbouring table, four pairs of eyes were closely watching my movements. With my confidence evaporating, I looked down at the noodles again and considered what I might have done wrong. Too much slurping perhaps, or not enough?

I had remembered to raise the bowl, my chopsticks were correctly positioned; the upper one held like a pencil one third of the way down; the other set against it, balanced between finger and thumb. Inexpert though I was, I hadn't lost control of them or let a noodle escape. What then?

'Hidari-kiki?' she asked. Smiling shyly, the mother nodded towards my still-suspended left hand. Hidari-kiki? Left-handed? Then it dawned on me. I was eating with my left hand in a country where less than ten percent of the population were lefties. Here the norm was right-handedness. Everything was designed to serve the right-handed population, from the ancient Japanese art of calligraphy to modern convenience. Whether executing a brush stroke in ink or operating a hot drink vending machine, you needed to use your right hand. So, while my perfect table manners had gone unnoticed, my left-handedness certainly hadn't.

See Japan and South Korea map on page 236.

Blushing Onions and
Therapy by the Sea

A blast on the foghorn is followed by an apologetic tinkle of music from the ship's intercom, waking its passengers from fitful sleep. The music stops, replaced by polite but firm messages. Their purpose is to eject us from our cabins, ready for disembarkation. I comply, removing myself quickly to escape more intrusion.

Stumbling up the stairs to deck six, I encounter returning French holidaymakers, already milling about with their luggage or in the queue for a quick petit dejeuner. I move through them and step outside to taste the sea tang and inhale some French air. We have arrived. Protesting like a blunt knife, the Plymouth to Roscoff cross-channel ferry judders as it carves a watery passage into port, through rolling morning mist and a swirl of aggrieved seagulls. After a moment, the curtain lifts to reveal a compact line of uneven granite buildings standing like a damp welcome committee on the Brittany shoreline.

We shuffle through passport control and customs, silent and dishevelled, to be cast out into the cold air of the ferry port. With the shadow of sleepiness still dogging me, I begin the slow walk up into the small town of Roscoff.

I am not expecting much—perhaps a harbour with a few fishing vessels and a café or two. The prospect feels underwhelming. In any case, I only have a few short hours on French soil before the return leg of the journey.

Gradually, the anonymous port buildings give way to a field of dew-dripping cabbages, announcing arrival in suburbia as we enter the Rue de Plymouth. A line of large detached houses sense us pass by from behind closed hostile shutters.

The mist has drenched everything in its path. In impeccably neat gardens, bedraggled rhododendron bushes sit motionless like plump glistening buddhas, and lanky hollyhocks droop their wet red flowers despondently. I too have been dunked in dampness and begin to wish I hadn't ignored the ship's call to breakfast. How long will I have to wait for a café to open, I wonder. But finally we reach the town's main thoroughfare, and there is one.

Moving figures and the hum of voices draw us in. Ty Pierre. It's already buzzing with locals. What does the name mean? For a fleeting moment I wonder if I have landed in a different country then realise that I am not reading French, but Breton.

I clear my throat and venture the question. The waitress pauses, café au lait in hand, thinks for a moment and then translates it back into French for me. It's simply Chez Pierre, or 'Pierre's Place'.

After ordering a coffee I pick up the local newspaper from the bar. My eyes fall on the lead story and its accompanying picture—a serious Frenchman staring straight at the camera. He's holding aloft a braid of reddish looking onions. Apparently, a fête de l'oignon has just taken place.

That explains the dozen or so cone-shaped tents we passed, standing forlornly in the Aire de Jeux park near the old port. Around them, a handful of workmen had been slowly dismantling, or stacking empty pallets. But why an onion festival? My interest piqued, I read on.

It seems that the pink onions of Roscoff are famous. Cultivated locally in a soil and climate which suits them, they generate a lucrative industry. The town chefs transform them into imaginative culinary delicacies, I discover, like lipig—even the sound sticks to my palate as I say it. This thick onion marmalade is the key ingredient of local preserves, soups, caramelised onion tart and other specialities.

Roscoff has been proudly showing off all facets of its celebrity vegetable over the weekend and the festival has attracted traders and growers from all over the region.

There is more. This humble onion has its own historical credentials, which led to an Anglo-French rapprochement. In the 1800s an enterprising Roscovite boarded a boat with his bicycle and crossed the channel in search of a new market for his onions. Dubbed 'Johnnie onion man', by his new Anglo-Saxon customers, his initiative resulted in an armada of peddling 'Johnnies' bringing the taste of France to English shores over the following centuries.

So, Roscoff knows about onions. A fishing village with an innovative sideline in a speciality bulb. The onion business diversified and even brings in some extra tourist revenue too, judging from the row of souvenir shops. The coffee and this discovery perks me up. With a better understanding of Roscoff under my belt, I leave Ty Pierre's to wander along the seafront. The mist has all but disappeared and the tide has ebbed, revealing a network of rockpools, lounging the length of the shore and draped in seductive green negligees of seaweedy fronds. These are releasing the unmistakeable scent of sea air. I turn a corner and make another discovery.

To complement its blushing bulbs, Roscoff has cashed in on the abundance of its seaweed resource and established itself as a centre of thalassotherapy. Since 1899, it has been a pioneering resort for sea cures and marine health products deriving from its mineral-rich seaweed and iodized sea air.

Offering body wraps of algae paste, sea fog inhalation and massages, thalassotherapy promises invigorating skin renewal and lung benefits. Becoming the centrepiece of a restorative wrap of seaweed paste sounds like an interesting experience, but my time on shore is almost over. Warmed by the afternoon sun, I walk slowly back down to the ferry, realising that Roscoff has surprised me. I will make a return visit one day.

See France map on page 244.

A Touch of the Scary

Something to Write Home About

A conspiracy of flies clusters on the quayside. A searing sun bears down on a new delivery of curled chicken feet, cartilage, beaks and bones. The flies are on the march now, crawling like small black infantrymen over plucked white wings and decapitated heads sporting pale pink combs. This delivery is destined for the cooking pot. Stock for the noodle soup tomorrow, perhaps, or served braised, on a bed of rice.

Nearby, slapping gently on the brown waters of the Tembeling river is the longboat that carried us here. It lies idle now after yesterday's heady ride through spuming rapids with a cargo of thrill-seeking passengers. We are staying at this camp, upriver in the verdant rainforest of Taman Negara National Park in Malaysia, where we have come in search of jungle adventure.

This morning we woke early and ascended Bukit Teresek to hear the gibbons calling from the hilltop. We took out a small recorder and held it high while the arboreal apes duetted across the canopy. The concert was as bewitching as a siren's song. Their eerie whoops echoed from tree to tree, gathering pace and reaching a spectacular screeching crescendo before fading away into a mournful murmur. There was no encore. We craned our necks but saw nothing. So, we played back their calls from the hissing tape recorder. It worked. The tricked gibbons came closer to peer out from their leafy sanctuary. Finding two non-simian imposters, they lost interest and crashed away through the branches. But it was enough. We caught a glimpse of their watchful faces and swinging limbs. Elated, we descended the hill back to camp.

Back at the quayside, we sit in the makeshift restaurant, eating fish and rice at a shaky bamboo table. A postcard, part-written, lies beside my plate. Close by is an old man in a straw hat working with a scythe, back bent as he sweeps the curved blade back and forth through the long lush grass. The sweet smell of mowing mingles with the sultry afternoon air. I pick at my bony fish. I decided this was a safer option than the chicken dish on the menu. Across the table, my companion scoops up a palmful of rice, adopting the local eating style with his right hand, fastidiously washed.

Suddenly, a Malay curse rings out. The table wobbles as I twist round, and in that instant, I see the rice grains tumble from my friend's cupped hand. There is a flurry of wild slashing from the shouting scythe operator. I am so close I could reach out and touch him, but I cringe away in shock. Abruptly, the swinging blade stops, and the man stands back, passing a damp arm across his brow. Then he tentatively extends the tip, teasing the grass open like a surgeon parting an incision. He lifts something out, held at arm's length. Two halves of a scaly brown and highly venomous pit viper dangle lifelessly from the blade. Under the table my toes clench in terror. Two chicken feet in open sandals beside the unfinished postcard, which has fluttered to the floor.

See Malaysia map on page 245.

A Ride into the Shadow Underworld

'Halloo, Mrs. Where you go? You wan' becak?' The Indonesian pedicab driver hails me, having pedalled up unnoticed behind his unwitting victim in this dusty backstreet.

'No, thanks. Jalan, jalan (I'm walking),' I reply, quickening my pace. But in the sultry heat of a tropical afternoon, my tired and weak legs are no match for his brown sinewy ones, and he is not going to be put off that easily.

I am in Jogja, as the locals affectionately call the royal city of Yogyakarta. It lies in the central province of Java, 550 kilometres east of Jakarta, and I'm taking a meandering route across the Indonesian archipelago, eastwards towards the islands of Bali and Lombok, seeing the sights as I go. Jogja is my halfway point.

Two days ago, feeling intrepid, I struggled up to the summit of nearby Mount Merapi, a smoking and volatile volcano, to see the sun rise over its fiery crater. Shooting stars accompanied me, dancing across the night sky. Below in the rich volcanic soil, field upon field of pungent tobacco plants grew. I had walked through them on my way to the volcano, feeling giddy and intoxicated by their overpowering scent. After the climb, the young boy guiding us back down had gently made fun of us as we stumbled along the path of lava fragments, losing our foothold on the scree. Giggling, he pointed to our legs and mimicked with his fingers, commenting, 'You walk like ant now.' So for the next two days I'm recovering my strength and dignity, and simply hanging loose in Jogja.

Just now, I have to admit I don't have a clue where I am in this clutter of small lookalike streets so I decide that resistance is not only futile but also counterproductive. I give in and accept the offer of a becak ride.

'Okay. To the Kraton Sultan's Palace, silhakan (please).' I clasp the strut supporting the flimsy roof of the vehicle and climb in, collapsing onto the hot plastic seat behind the driver. Five minutes of no-sweat pedal power later (I am a light load), he drops me in a courtyard in front of the red-roofed palace and I pay up. I am surprised when he hands me a scrappy bit of paper in return. His business card, maybe? No. Peering at it, I see that it's an illegible address, scribbled in fading biro.

'You like Wayang kulit? Jogja famous. Bagus (Very good). You come see. Seven o'clock. Special price for you.' He grins, taking my non-committal shrug as agreement, then he pedals off to find another customer.

That evening I surprise myself and follow up on the invitation. Indecipherable though it is to me, the piece of paper holds no coded enigma for the next becak driver. I find him sleeping in the back of his vehicle outside Guest House Hibiscus where I'm staying. We set off. Rattling over the dark potholed street, the becak shakes me about like a bean in a tin can, and with each new jolt I wonder if I have made the right decision. The unlit house where I am deposited twenty minutes later does not look particularly welcoming or even inhabited. For the second time that day, I have no idea where I am.

'Here, Mrs. This place. Terima kasih (Thank you).' And he too pedals away. It does not feel quite right. I hesitate in front of the entrance—a small porch with a broken roof and steps that lead down to a wooden door. It's closed. There is no sound from inside. It doesn't resemble any of the usual tourist venues. Suddenly, the door swings open; a draped mosquito net parts and a woman's arm extends and pulls me forward, 'Salamat datang! Welcome! Wayang kulit, yes? Please come.'

I follow her and we descend more steps into a basement. Yes, I am here for Wayang kulit, Indonesian shadow puppet theatre; a recommended cultural highlight of any visit to Jogja. And I see that I'm not alone. The basement is bursting with an audience in waiting. A faint smell of sweat hangs over the dark room and the eyes in the faces of the twenty or so people sitting cross-legged on its floor are alight with expectation. Indonesian devotees of this ancient art sit alongside curious foreigners. I find a small space and crouch down, arranging my legs into a comfortable position.

In front of us stands a large white canvas screen, backlit and empty. To the left sits an orchestra—a line of four gamelan players, all men, dressed in traditional batik jackets, sarongs and headdress. They sit, calm and poised before their instruments, ready to provide the music to accompany the show. I can see bronze gongs and cymbals of varying sizes, a xylophone, a leather-topped drum and a bamboo flute.

I am looking around at my fellow spectators when a hush suddenly descends on the room. The music starts up. It is immediately strange, a jangling and discordant sound. I concentrate, trying to discern a rhythm, but the chimes and bongs assault my unaccustomed westerner's ears.

Then a shrill commanding voice replaces the music and the shadow profiles of two stick-like human figures with bulbous heads move slowly across the screen towards each other. The performance has begun. The puppet handlers kneel, behind, out of sight, below the screen, and dexterously manipulate the rods attached to their puppets' long skinny limbs. The figures shake and quiver into life. Beaky-nosed and bulging-eyed characters, they are hunched and grotesque. These are the stuff of nightmares. I have read that they are based on stories from ancient Hindu epics which the storyteller embellishes with political, humorous or philosophical twists to delight his domestic audience. The puppets are all equipped with long menacing fingers that wave and point as the story unfolds. Some represent fools or heroes; others, strange gods or demons, but I am the stranger here and cannot tell the good guys from the bad guys. I watch in wonder, buoyed along by the jerking shadows and the jarring music but comprehending nothing. I am uncertain where all this will lead and lost without translation. It is another becak ride into the unknown.

Time passes; the shadow puppets come and go. There are interactions between them, but I cannot tell whether they reflect harmony or conflict. Without warning, the music starts to gain momentum, and I sense we are reaching the climax. It culminates in a clanging crescendo and stops, dead. The drama is over. On the screen, the villain has been dispatched and all that is left is a fallen shadow with the victorious hero bending over him, or so I surmise. I may be wrong. The puppet master and his assistants step out from behind the screen and take a bow. One of them, I know. It is my first driver from earlier that day. Becak driver by day, puppet handler by night. Silently, the audience files out and climbs the steps. At the door the draped mosquito net parts again and the woman bids us 'Selamat Malam (Good night),' as we are released from this netherworld. It feels strangely liberating to breathe the warm evening air again.

See Indonesia map on page 246.

Night Fright

I could have stayed on the bus and continued inland all the way up to the Lasithi Plateau, but I didn't. A big mistake. It was never part of my plan to make an overnight stop in Ayios Nikolaos. I don't think I'll ever know what impulse made me get off here.

It's April 1992 and, for the last week or so, I've been galivanting across Crete, the largest of the Greek islands, from one end to the other on a botanical quest. The spring flowers, especially the wild orchids, are at their best and I've scoured the Cretan hills in search of them. Small and elusive, many with intricate flowers that expertly mimic their insect pollinators, I'm having a dizzy holiday romance with orchids and am in floral heaven here. I know them all intimately, by their Latin names as well as their common ones: the tongue orchid, the naked-man orchid, milky orchid, the mirror orchid, the rare Cretan bee orchid. I could go on. These and other new finds are now ticked off from my orchid twitcher's list. Wandering eastwards, I've embraced most of Crete's archaeological sites, looking down on them as I roam the flower-filled hillsides. From above there are breathtaking views of the Minoan Palace of Knossos and the Roman remains of Gortyna. It's been a perfect trip—until today.

The departing bus gives a dry farewell cough of exhaust fumes as I look around, and the magnitude of my mistake sinks in. In Ayios Nikolaos I've stumbled upon the mecca of package tourism. It's teeming with tack; a sextuplet of souvenir shops lines one side of the street, while opposite I see a row of slouching tavernas, each displaying a billboard with an English menu and peeling photos of unappetising meatballs and chips.

On the waterfront it's no better. A string of monochrome hotels, stripped of their Greek identity, are awaiting the next pre-booked coach party. And to my dismay, when I check their room prices, I find they are twice as expensive as anywhere else in Crete. Nothing here for my budget so I set off towards the newly opened youth hostel.

It's a long walk out of town. Ayios Nikolaos is expanding, and its eastern perimeter is a construction site. Bands of concrete development stretch out greedily to smother the pristine coast and taint the turquoise sea. Next to a vacant lot of rubble and wasteland, I find the new hostel I am looking for, with its shutters down.

Yiorgos, the manager, is just leaving. Seeing me approach, he lifts his head upwards in a half nod and gives a click of his tongue. A bad sign. It's the Greek way of conveying a negative. And, in case I'm in any doubt, 'Ochi. No room. We close for Pascha.' Pascha—the Greek Orthodox Easter! I had forgotten. It's this weekend.

I plead, first in English and then try a little Greek, 'Parakalo (please),' pointing to the heavy backpack I have been carrying from the town centre. Yiorgos continues padlocking the gate and repeats the tongue clicking. I stand my ground and in the end my stubbornness pays off. He wants to leave but reluctantly opens the gate again and books me in for the night, warning me that there will be no breakfast and only cold water to shower with tomorrow. I shrug; it doesn't matter. I will be leaving early in the morning. But a shadow of doubt clouds this thought as I wonder about the impact of Orthodox Easter. A premonition that things may not go to plan. Without a backward glance, Yiorgos drives off to spend the Easter weekend with his family, and I am left alone.

As dusk starts to fall, I sit out on the still-warm concrete balcony that surrounds the hostel's upper floor. My field guide to the wild orchids of Crete is open on my lap. Behind me is the dormitory. I have it entirely to myself, I think, smugly.

My stomach interrupts with a question. I have neglected it but there is no chance of a meal in a taverna unless I want to walk several kilometres back into town. Wait a minute, though… I retrieve two squashed Greek pies from the bottom of my backpack. On inspection, one turns out to be a tiropita minus most of its cheese, which has oozed out. I prefer not to think where. I choose the other, a spanakopita, still with its spinach filling intact. I take a bite and start reading about the orchids that are still to be hunted down.

Later I test all the dorm beds, scoring their mattresses for comfort and unroll my sleeping bag on the winner. I am just drifting off to sleep when a noise jerks me upright. Did I imagine it? I strain to listen, but only the darkness breathes a heavy silence. Then it comes again. It's from somewhere outside. A strange drawn-out, brushing sound, like someone slipping down—or shinning up—a drainpipe. But who or what is it? And where is it coming from? My hands ball up tensely beside me and I sit rigid, forcing myself to search for a rational explanation.

Could it be the owl I heard hooting as I laid out my sleeping bag, landing on its prey, perhaps? No, wrong sound. A fox scavenging in the bins? I didn't see any bins. Is the place haunted? It's a new building. Surely not. Whoever heard of a haunted youth hostel? The scraping sound comes again and from somewhere close by. The balcony? I stare at the double wooden doors, which I've left slightly ajar to cool the room's interior and let in a little moonlight. I can't see anything beyond, but there is something or somebody out there, just a few metres away. I'm sure of it. I hear the sound again. Is it someone moving along and trying different doors to see if one of them is open?

Shakily, I ease the zipper of my sleeping bag down, inch by inch, until I can move my legs out and onto the stone floor. I feel for my folded trousers, which were serving as a lumpy makeshift pillow. Then I hold my breath as I pull them on and pick up my walking boots. My body is adrenaline-charged now and, in an instant, I am dressed and standing beside the bed, boots in one hand and with my sleeping bag squeezed into my backpack, ready to flee in response to primal fear.

I blink and remain motionless as I realise that my exit is blocked. The stairs down to the ground floor are accessed from outside. I would need to pass along the connected balconies first. I'm trapped. Outside in the silence someone is waiting for me, ready to pounce. In my bare feet, I creep over the cool tiles to the back of the dormitory and crouch down behind the farthest bed, placing my backpack and boots protectively in front of me. More questions come that I don't have answers to. Can I be seen from here? What should I do next?

Agitation is now swirling the spinach pie around my stomach. I try to calm myself with deep breaths and by imagining myself somewhere else: the Lasithi Plateau. I'm breathing in the clear air, sitting outside a kafenio in a picturesque village, digesting a hearty Greek supper and feeling good about life. I should be there now. Why did I get off that bus? I lay my head on top of my backpack. The balcony has gone quiet. Stay alert, an inner voice urges me. I take more deep breaths.

Hours later I wake, as the first rays of light reach across the floor from between the balcony doors. I am still hunkered down behind the bed with an aching neck and stiff bent legs. I raise my head from my backpack. I can hear the birds enthusiastically delivering their uncoordinated morning chorus outside. Nothing happened. It was a lucky escape—whoever it was must have thought that the hostel was empty and left long ago. It seems safe now.

I cautiously stand up, flex my shoulders and walk out onto the balcony. It's empty. The birds continue their singing, and the view is still of the rubble-strewn wasteland below. I feel reassured. Returning inside, I pull on my boots, gather my belongings and exit via the balcony to descend the stairs, ignoring the shower room as I pass it.

It is as I am leaving the hostel that I notice him. Lying on the concrete floor near the entrance is a scruffy dog. The mongrel guardian of the hostel while his master is away. On seeing me he raises himself unsteadily on three legs. The fourth hangs limply behind. I rummage in my pack for the remains of the cheese tiropita and throw it on the ground. With a feeble wag of his tail, he hobbles towards it, dragging his damaged appendage across the concrete. As he does so, his gnarled claws come into contact with the surface and there is a long scraping sound.

See Greece, Crete, Turkey, Egypt and Israel map on page 243.

A Walk on the Wild Side

I should never have listened to him in the first place. My companion Jordi's latest suggestion may well make matters worse. 'We'll hide,' he announces, 'and pretend we're commandos.' I can tell that he is relishing the prospect.

It's not a good idea. I am sure of this. And I suspect I will lack any aptitude for commando impersonation. I let out a sigh. What we have set out to do has already not gone to plan. And this new suggestion may have other unforeseen consequences.

The year is 1991 and we are in Tuscany in the glorious springtime, holidaying a few kilometres above a promontory on the west coast of Italy, and not far from the border with Umbria. For several days we have enjoyed idyllic scenes of gently rolling hills, of carefully tended vineyards and olive groves, all bathed in a rich buttery light. Scenes of the kind seen on the double page spreads of magazines left lying in dentists' waiting rooms: snapshots of cultivated Italian countryside dotted with picturesque villas, cradled between lines of flaming cypress trees. Paradise.

But we know that this is not the only kind of Tuscan landscape. There is a wilder untamed side to this region, and, this morning, in Grosseto, we boarded a blue Linea 7 bus to take us into the regional park of the Maremma where we hope to find it.

A chain of hills bristling with pine forest, the Monti dei Uccellini, forms the undulating backbone of this protected area for wildlife, extending over 24,000 acres. Topped by ruined watchtowers built during the Spanish occupation, these hills are aptly named the 'mountains of little birds' and overlook a vast swathe of umbrella pines, which gradually thins out and merges into maquis scrubland. This, in turn, gives way to sand dunes and culminates in a beach, caressed by the waters of the Mediterranean. This is the wilder side of Tuscany that we want to explore.

After half an hour or so the route 7 bus deposits us at a park entry point in the coastal town of Albarese. Opposite the bus stop stands a small kiosk, the ticket office, with its slatted brown shutter unfavourably pulled down. We cross the street to inspect it. In case we require further confirmation, there it is: a sign hanging in front announcing that it is *chiuso*. The day's first setback.

The tourist information in Grosseto was unequivocal—the park would certainly be open as the spring season has started. So why is it closed now? We linger beside it, feeling irritated and disappointed at the same time. Then we notice two uniformed park rangers sitting in the sun and drinking coffee outside a bar near the bus stop. We cross the street again and seek their help.

'Si Senora, è chiuso. Oggi è aperto solo per i tour prenotati. (Yes Madam, it's closed. It's only open for booked tours today).' They smile and sip their espressos. Needing to vent our frustration, we appeal, and press our case in true Italian style, arguing for special permission to enter the park having travelled a long way and so on, but it is all to no effect. They are very sorry but insist that we should come back tomorrow. We turn and walk away. Jordi is already hatching plan B. An hour later we are inside the park, having entered illegally by walking along the beach at its open north-west perimeter. Our first mistake.

'We can always say that we crossed into it without knowing,' Jordi reassures me, sensing my anxiety. I frown. Will this excuse really wash with a shrewd Italian park ranger? And what if we bump into the same pair from the café? But it is too late now. I have meekly followed Jordi and can only take comfort from that fact that there is no sign of anyone else in the park, let alone any tour groups.

We turn inland trying to keep away from the footpaths where we might risk an encounter; instead, we walk among the juniper trees where the sand is criss-crossed with deer tracks. Ducking to avoid the dry lower branches, we brush our way through. At our feet, black dung beetles with furrowed backs are scuttling about like tipsy mountaineers, losing their footing on the unstable sandy terrain. Occasional clumps of half-hidden orchids—white helleborines—poke out from behind the tree trunks to surprise us.

The air is full of birdsong. A cuckoo, an early spring visitor to western Italy, is persistently calling for attention somewhere nearby. Perhaps it has already laid its eggs sneakily in the nest of a local magpie.

We walk on, the vegetation becoming denser, and the soft, shifting sand replaced by a single layer of dry pine needles. They give off their resinous fragrance as we crush them underfoot. Small outcrops of rock begin to appear, and we scramble up one of them to get a better view.

Looking down over the pines, we fantasize that there may be fat crested porcupines waddling about below. They have been introduced to Italy from Africa by the Romans and there is evidence that some are here. In the undergrowth we have found their distinctive calling cards, the striped quills they shed as they shamble along. Under certain trees there are also signs of wild boar, the churned-up troughs of soil where they have grubbed for bulbs and tubers.

Immersed in the wildlife, we don't hear the approaching tour group until they are almost upon us, high voices and light laughter breaking through the birdsong like a bubbling spring. It is a party of excited Italian school children—a booked tour group—and they are on the path just below. A ranger is leading them.

Any minute they will see us! I look around for a hole that might obligingly swallow me up. But Jordi, rising to the challenge, goes into commando mode. In the absence of suitable holes, I can only follow his lead. I become a reluctant rookie in this next mad scheme.

'Get down or they'll see us!' he hisses. This is easier said than done but I obey and try to crouch behind a rock. I feel sure I am visible—a very conspicuous and panicky human blot on the landscape. What if they do see us? Will we be thrown out of the park in disgrace or even arrested?

The pine needle dust is in danger of making me sneeze and my skin is being assaulted by the sharp spines of scrub-loving bushes, rock shards or, maybe, biting ants. I lie clutching the ground and trying to locate where the group is from the sound of their voices. The park ranger has stopped on the path and is addressing the children. He is telling them about the wildlife in the park. I catch a single word, echoed enthusiastically by one of the children, 'tartaruga (tortoise)!' We have already encountered several today. Disturbed by us, they moved surprisingly quickly, often wedging themselves fast into clefts between the white rocks, presenting their impenetrable shells like the defensive shields of Roman legionaries. I look around for some large rocks where I might try wedging myself, tortoise-style. My heart is still pounding like a pneumatic drill on a concrete pavement. Do real commandos get stressed like this?

Suddenly, Jordi's voice breaks through the sound of my palpitations, 'It's okay, they've gone.' He is grinning.

Mercifully, we have escaped detection. I scramble upright and brush the dirt and vegetation from my clothes. The group are now some way off, their voices very faint. I feel drained and as if I my skin has been massaged with a porcupine, but now, at least, I am back in the world I prefer to inhabit.

'Let's go,' I say firmly. 'I've had enough adventures for one day.'

Later, restored by a glass of cold beer in the bar by the bus stop, we reflect on the day's events as we wait for the bus to return us to Grosseto. I doubt I could ever hack it as a real commando, but playing the role for a short while saved the day. I am unlikely to forget my walk on the wild side of Tuscany.

See Italy map on page 240.

Crossings

Borderland

We sit, warm and dry, inside the wood-panelled living room of Gasthaus Hofer. Around us, items of carved Bavarian furniture with clawed feet, solid and rather intimidating, display a collection of floral china and ceramic beer steins. We are watching, in a disinterested way, as crooked streaks of rainwater engage in a stop-start race down the windowpane. For two days now we have been waiting for the rain to stop. Months ago, in holiday-planning mode, I imagined myself walking in the Bavarian Forest with bright summer sunshine spangling down through the trees around me. It turned out to be a pipe dream. I hadn't allowed for leaden skies and heavy downpours in southern Germany in mid-August.

The Bayerischer Wald sounded exotic—one hundred kilometres of wooded hills meandering beside the border with the Czech Republic. Over on the Czech side, the Bohemian Forest, known as Šumava, mirrors its progress closely. We are visiting both forests using the small German town of Zwiesel as our base.

Zwiesel lies just fifteen kilometres from the border. It owes its name to the fork of a river, which it straddles. The two parts are called the Grosser Regen and Kleiner Regen (Big Rain and Little Rain). These weren't the only warnings we received of

Bavaria's meteorological unpredictability in summertime. On the way here, driving through open hills and lush meadowland, we passed the towns of Regensburg and Regen. Picture-perfect places that welcome their visitors with flower-filled troughs and balconies and squares that are spotlessly clean and tidy. But the irony of these names only dawns on us now as we stare out at the wet world beyond the painted shutters.

Coo-coo; coo-coo; coo-coo. An authentic but very irritating Bavarian cuckoo clock on the wall of our chalet startles us both as it announces the late morning hour. We turn away from the window.

'Come on. Let's go out; we can look for blueberries in the forest.' My Czech friend has also had enough of watching rain-water run.

It's not a bad idea, all things considered, so we don walking boots, waterproof jackets and trousers and prepare to go blue-berry-picking in the pouring rain.

To be fair to the weather, it hasn't rained every day of our holiday. The first few days were overcast but mostly dry. Two days ago, on our first foray into the Bavarian Forest, we found an abundance of fungi sprouting from soil and tree. Like many of his countrymen, my companion is a connoisseur in this department and an expert at hunting down edible mushrooms. By the end of the first morning, we had a haul to rival those of the suppliers of London's top restaurants.

But we weren't looking for a lucrative market. Instead, we took them back to our small kitchenette in Gasthaus Hofer and rustled up a menu of mushroom dishes. Sparassis crispa mit eiern became our signature dish. Cauliflower fungus with eggs—scrambled eggs. We had found a large clump of this gastronomic prize in excellent condition. With a head resembling an enormous spikey cauliflower, it took a long time to remove the plant debris from its many branched lobes but eventually our trophy was ready for the pan. Its sweet earthy aroma almost made me swoon with hunger as we waited impatiently for it to cook through. We agreed that it was one of the most flavourful mushroom dishes either of us had ever eaten.

But on the following day the clouds began to gather ominously like a battalion of grey tanks preparing for an invasion. We fled eastwards across the border hoping they would not follow us. We were going to take a closer look at Czech Šumava.

'Does it have any meaning?' I asked my friend. 'I mean the forest's name, Šumava.'

He considered for a moment before answering, 'I think it comes from the Czech word, šumění to describe the sound wind makes in the trees.'

'Yes. Shhhh-umava.' I repeated. It had a lovely onomatopoeic ring to it, and I could imagine a forest full of singing trees. But would it be different from its German neighbour? I wondered. Together, the forests formed the largest area of wilderness in Central Europe and presumably had much in common.

That day we wandered on the other side of the border, through the Bohemian Forest. Much of it was spruce plantation. Neat rows of tall evergreen trees, their branches laden with light brown cones, stretched in all directions, but there was no wind, so the Czech trees did not sing for us. It all seemed quite similar to the forest on the German side.

Then we made a strange discovery. Not far from the border, cutting a swathe through the spruce, was a wide band of cropped grass, devoid of trees. It couldn't be natural, but what was it? We walked along its course until we found an explanation. Knee-high concrete pyramids on the grass and rusty metal spikes, standing ready like giant jacks in a game of five stones, betrayed something more sinister. Behind them, inconspicuously grassed over, were artificial earthworks.

Pointing to the earthworks, my friend explained: 'These are military posts from the Communist time—the soldiers hid inside them. They were waiting to shoot anyone who tried to cross the border to go to the West. The people thought they would get caught in the forest behind and were very scared. But the soldiers didn't bother making patrols there. They were just sitting and waiting for them here where they had to cross the place with no trees.'

We stood in silence. Two forest hikers looking at these ghostly reminders of the Iron Curtain era. The border between Czechoslovakia and West Germany had been heavily guarded during the Cold War. This chilling place where many people had lost their lives while trying to escape to the West was as quiet as a graveyard now.

Dark clouds had gathered over Šumava and it was starting to rain. Our mood had changed too, so we decided to return to our parked car. On the way we passed a very inconspicuous sign in Czech, next to a small wet ditch in the forest floor.

I looked to my companion for a translation. Despite our recent discovery, he became quite animated: 'It's the source of the Vltava, here in the forest!' This time we had stumbled upon a Czech national treasure.

The Vltava, the longest river in the Czech Republic, runs all the way from southern Bohemia to Prague, where it passes under the capital's many bridges and beyond. The fame of the country's national river grew even more when the Czech composer, Smetana, charted its course in the music of his composition, Má Vlast (My Country).

That patch of damp earth at our feet, barely a spring, was the source of one of its two headstreams, the sign informed us. It lightened our mood, but the rain was falling harder so we hurried back across the border to Zwiesel and Gasthaus Hofer, where some generous slices of Prinzregententorte lay waiting for us.

That was two days ago. We brought the rain back with us across the border. Now we've had enough of sitting indoors rain-watching, and only crumbs remain of the Bavarian layered chocolate cake.

So, under a steady downpour, we venture out and set about collecting blueberries, of which there are an abundance in the Bavarian Forest. They will add some pizzazz to our morning muesli. We find a bush laden with fat blue berries, freshly washed by the rain, and start to fill our containers. Large plops of water land on our hooded heads as we work.

Despite my waterproofs, the rainwater has seeped under the cuffs of my jacket, soaking my wrists. Our hands are cold and blotchy, fingers numb. My trousers prevent the water reaching my legs but create a perfect conduit for it to run off into my boots, trickling its way between eyelets and laces to soak my socks. I flex a foot tentatively and feel it squelch within my boot. Yuk!

The bush has been plucked almost bare of berries now, so I leave my Czech friend to finish off and move on through the trees to the next clearing in search of a new bush to plunder. Then, I stop in surprise. I have stepped into an Alice in Wonderland moment. Not a White Rabbit apparition, but two gangly-limbed, wet hares with saucer-like eyes and sodden ears.

And I can't quite believe what I am seeing. The animals are leaping about ecstatically in a rain dance, sending splashes of water up into the air. A celebration reminiscent of Gene Kelly in the pavement scene of *Singin' in the Rain*. Suddenly alarmed by my intrusion, they bound away into the forest and the magical moment evaporates. The spell is broken and, amazingly, in the sky above me, a small patch of blue is showing through the clouds. It looks as if the sun will come out on both sides of the border tomorrow.

See Germany, Czech Republic and Hungary map on page 247.

A Case of Fishy Synchronicity

S itting in the Lucky Cat kissaten, I explain my problem. My Japanese friend and I are the only customers in the coffee shop in downtown Toyohashi in Aichi prefecture. 'Sou desu ka (I see),' he nods gravely, giving nothing away, and then falls silent.

I study the cartoon cat on my coffee cup closely as I wait for more. It's a maneki-neko, a cat with a raised paw and a symbol of good luck here. With impeccable Japanese courtesy, the reply comes and, with it, a solution: 'Julie-san, maybe you could go to Shimonoseki port. There is bullet train from Nagoya. After you can take boat to Busan, South Korea and train to Seoul capital. There, go to Japanese embassy for new visa in passport. Maybe this is short and best way.'

It sounds like good advice. I have entered Japan on a sixty-day tourist visa in the summer of 1979, but my plan is to stay for two years. With the appropriate paperwork I could get a different kind of visa. One that will allow me a longer stay and permission to engage in what, translated from the Japanese, are called 'cultural activities'.

Taking the land and sea route to South Korea to effect this change of status holds a certain appeal. And it would make an interesting start to whatever cultural activities might follow. October is also the perfect time to see a highly celebrated event in this part of East Asia: the leaves changing colour. An autumn phenomenon that even has its own name, I discovered. The Japanese refer to it as Momiji while the Koreans call it the Danpoong. So, my problem is solved. I pack my camera, guidebook and a small suitcase.

One super-fast train ride later, the Shinkansen from Nagoya arrives precisely on time in Shimonoseki station, gliding in like a blunt-nosed silver pencil. Located at the western end of Honshu, the largest of Japan's four main islands, Shimonoseki is a port famous for its seafood, especially blowfish, or fugu as it is called in Japanese. This is a fish that exerts a powerful and dangerous fascination in both Japan and South Korea.

As I have a few hours to kill before the departure of the ferry for Busan, I decide to visit the most likely place to see fugu: the local fish market. It is not difficult to find. I follow my nose from a nearby street where a permeating whiff of fish suggests that I am on the right track. Inside, the market is heaving with people and fish.

Water is sloshing everywhere, flooding the wet stone slabs. Iridescent fish scales glitter among the rows of neatly laid out piscine specimens. Each row of fish bears a label stating its name in bold black kanji—but I can't decipher the Japanese characters to read them. Behind are brimming glass tanks, spilling water on all sides. Their live occupants are jostling for space as they peer out at the strange new world now surrounding them.

I look back at the slabs. I know red snapper and yellowtails are local specialities that will be here somewhere and try to guess which fish they might be. One candidate for the red snapper is a pop-eyed rosy specimen. Blushing coyly out from its place in the row, it seems quite attractive until I catch a glimpse of its distinctive teeth—all the better to snap you with!

And the yellowtails must be those silvery-white torpedoes with bright yellow fins and tails. But where are the infamous blowfish? My eyes move up and down the rows and catch the attention of the fishmonger. He regards me quizzically. What is this foreigner looking for?

Tentatively, I try out my Japanese, 'Fugu arimasu-ka? (Do you have blowfish?)' With a wave of his filleting knife, he gestures towards one of the tanks, where some inoffensive-looking fish are swimming about lazily. Their chubby flanks are mottled with spots of greenish yellow and each has a creamy white underbelly. One has its round face pressed up against the glass and, with pursed lips, is contentedly blowing kisses to the outside world.

It doesn't look like a ruthless killer to me but, by all accounts, has been responsible for countless deaths among those who have dared to make a meal of it without due care and attention. In Japan only specially licensed chefs are allowed to prepare blowfish for restaurant consumption; the reason being, that parts of it, particularly the liver, contain a deadly poison. If eaten by mistake, they paralyse the diner and cause a slow death from asphyxiation. There is no known antidote.

I study the cherubic face on the other side of the glass. It is certainly a friendly-looking fugu, but its looks are deceptive, and, disturbingly, it seems to be returning my respectful interest with a look of tender affection. Feeling slightly unnerved, I turn back to the vendor who is trying to point me in the direction of a licensed restaurant where I can eat this national delicacy. With no time for dinner, and a reluctance to dice with death before changing my visa, I decline, as politely as I can, and hurry away to find the port and my ferry to Busan.

The two-hundred-kilometre journey across the straits to South Korea involves a long night crossing. The boat is crowded with Korean families returning home, laden with shopping and luggage, and losing excited children in all directions. Each family group eventually settles down to occupy an allocated floor space in the ship's main lounge.

They come well prepared and lay out assorted foil-wrapped packages of cold cooked rice, fish and fermented vegetables, before sharing out a pile of blankets for the coming night. I fall asleep with the smell of pickled cucumber in my nostrils. When I wake, the next morning, the lounge is empty. Only the floor is strewn with crumpled balls of foil and used chopsticks. The families are already queueing with their baggage to disembark.

The chilled early morning air of an October day induces shivers in me as we file through customs and immigration. Eventually, with my passport scrutinised and stamped, I am cast out into the streets of Busan. There is little sign of life, but

I suppose that the morning commute will start soon and fill the streets with scurrying workers.

I set off towards the railway station to find a train to take me northwards to the capital, but turning a corner, I come to an abrupt standstill. A large military tank is occupying the middle of the road, with the barrel of its gun pointing straight at me.

There is no sign of anyone inside the vehicle, although I strongly sense that I am being watched. Uncertain what to do, and slightly fearful that the tank turret and gun will swivel to follow me, I decide to continue walking, clutching my small suitcase defensively at my side. I hope this will convey the message that I am just a harmless tourist. But what is a tank doing in downtown Busan? Does the proximity of the port require a military presence? I don't know and am relieved to see the station come into view at the end of the next block.

The fast train to Seoul takes several hours. I pass the time flipping between the pages of my guidebook as I try to identify the best place to experience the Dan-poong. There are few people on the train, and, compared with the families on the boat, my fellow train passengers all seem very subdued.

More unsettling experiences await me in the capital. Outside the station, a group of Korean teenagers, dressed austerely in black school uniforms with white collars and few other trimmings, are huddled together like a cluster of dejected magpies. Some of them are crying. I stare in surprise while other Korean passers-by walk on paying no attention.

Noticing the foreigner watching them, two school children approach me and attempt to say something in broken English. 'Our president,' one sobs, followed by something unintelligible. I regret that I have no Korean vocabulary that might help elicit more.

They point to the black ribbons pinned to their chests and I catch another phrase, 'he die.' Then, 'last night dinner.' This brings on a further outbreak of tears and exchanges in Korean as they comfort each other. I am baffled and express my condolences as best I can but come away with only fragments of an understanding. The president is dead, and it has something to do with last night's dinner. Has he died while dining?

Then the neural networks in my brain snap into overdrive and a bubble surfaces somewhere in my hippocampus, bursting into a fleeting image of a pair of sweetly pursed fish lips. With it comes an awful thought. But surely that would be too much of a coincidence? Even so, blowfish is a speciality here and would certainly feature on a menu for a presidential dinner. Thank goodness I resisted the temptation to try it in Shimonoseki. It all seems a bit surreal.

I feel a sudden urge to leave the capital, but I need to settle the matter of my visa first. So, that afternoon, I go directly to the Japanese embassy, where I find the heavy-duty embassy doors inexplicably shut and locked. I check. It is a weekday, and the sign outside indicates that it should be open for business. I hover on the embassy steps for a time wondering what to do next. There is something altogether disconcerting about this trip.

As I stand fretting, I become aware of another western face passing by in the street. Its owner, who turns out to be an American student, stops when he sees me. My own face must be a picture of confusion, and he asks where I am from and whether I need help.

Yes, the embassy is shut, as is everything today, he explains. The whole country is on edge because of what happened to President Park last night. Hadn't I heard about his death at the presidential banquet? My mind races. So, I had understood the school children correctly.

'Was it the fish?' I blurt out. The American regards me askance for a moment, 'Fish? What fish? One of his aides pulled out a gun and shot him.'

The truth, it turns out, is almost stranger than my fishy fiction. President Park, an army general installed as the country's leader after a military coup, has himself been assassinated by his military colleague, Kim, director of the Korean intelligence agency, during a formal banquet. By the end of that fateful dinner, at least six people including the president and his bodyguard were lying dead in a pool of blood. All this happened last night as my ferry sailed calmly across the straits from Japan.

The next day, order is re-established in the country and the Japanese embassy opens up for business again. I change my visa and leave Seoul quickly to escape to the tranquillity of the mountains and the Dan-poong.

I never did find out why President Park Chung-hee was murdered during dinner on the night of the 26th October 1979.

Theories abound to this day—an attempted coup, a conspiracy, an impulsive act inspired by jealousy or desire for revenge. For me, the real reason didn't matter. I much prefer the explanation that my overactive brain, fuddled by fish encounters and inexplicable events, had concocted for his untimely death a story with an amorous blowfish cast as the unlikely assassin.

See Japan and South Korea map on page 236.

Footloose in the Jungle

The house geckos kept me awake. They are always squabbling on my ceiling in the middle of the muggy night. Two engaged in a head-to-head lacertilian scrap, hanging upside down from their Velcro-like toe-pads. There were dire consequences for the one that lost its footing and fell onto the rotating ceiling fan. I found its sliced body in a bloody splat on the floor the next morning.

This is not the first time I have had a grievance with the geckos. Earlier this week another rushed headlong into my fridge as I opened it, taking refuge in the vegetable tray at the bottom. Swearing, I emptied the fridge and made a grab for it. I was rewarded with a twitching tail in the hand as it made a leap for freedom. Since then, this tail-less creature has taunted me from wall and ceiling, its jerking head issuing threats of vengeance in my direction. I am looking forward to the weekend and an escape from the gecko wars at home.

The small sultanate of Brunei, tucked onto the edge of the vast tropical island of Borneo, is my home for seven months. I am living in the capital working as an expatriate teacher in a school. It is no ordinary secondary school, but one built on stilts over a water village standing in the Brunei river estuary. We teachers live on the mainland, and each morning we clamber into an open speedboat, our river taxi, to make the journey over to Kampung Air, the water village. We try not to get our smart school clothes too splashed by the spray as the motorboat whips across the water.

The water village, like Brunei itself, is a strange mix of the old world and the new. Fishermen and their families live in traditional rickety wooden homes on stilts over the water too. This community goes back generations, descended from the first coastal colonisers from the Malay peninsula. But, nowadays, these people are connected to the power grid and their homes are furnished with all the electrical mod cons and gadgetry that the residents of an oil-rich state can buy.

While the water village children study in the stilted school, when the tide is out the catfish crawl over the exposed mud, just as their Devonian ancestors did. Once, as I watched from above, the catfish were joined by a prehistoric monitor lizard, which had lumbered out of the forest. For a time, it slouched around among the muddy stilts, breathing heavily and drooling goblets of toxic saliva while daily lessons continued above.

But, this weekend, I am escaping my school duties and crossing the border from Brunei to the neighbouring Malaysian state of Sarawak. And I am travelling in the traditional way here: on foot and through the jungle. The idea of international travel without the need of a plane or ship appeals to me, even though my city-slicking students strongly advise against setting foot in the jungle. 'No good, Teacher. Jungle dangerous place!' they warn me.

Brunei's western border lies somewhere within the primary rainforest that sprawls like a dark ink splatter where the two countries meet.

'It'll take you about six hours,' a fellow teacher advises. 'There's a log walk—the locals use it to bring stuff across to trade.'

'A log walk?' I repeat, hoping for more information. He explains.

Through the wettest part of the jungle the path is replaced by a line of felled tree trunks, laid end to end over the swamp. Nevertheless, it is a well-established walking trail, that will eventually lead to a cold beer in a bar in the town of Marudi, in alcohol-permissive Sarawak. It is a route forbidden by the Bruneian authorities to foreigners, but the temptation is too great for many of us. 'Look out for the longhouse,' he adds.

So, that weekend I drive out with another teacher, for an hour and a half, along a straight coastal road from the capital. Passing a herd of dark satanic nodding donkeys, the offshore oil pumps of Shell, on the seaside, and a patchwork of rice paddies on the land side, we come to Labi, a small community in the far west corner of Brunei. Then, for the last mile or so, we are forced to slow down to a winding crawl along a pot-holed dirt track that runs parallel to the first outstretched finger of primary Bornean rainforest.

As our car carefully negotiates the deep craters, a pig-tailed macaque monkey saunters out of the forest to squat, bemused, in front of this strange slow-moving beast. For us, it is another obstacle to drive around, but we finally reach the end of the road and of the country. There, as expected, we find the longhouse with its backdrop of wall-to-wall jungle. It is the home of an extended Iban family, one of the indigenous peoples of Borneo, and we have been told we should pay them a visit.

A pack of dusty pigs, dogs and chickens are the first to greet us noisily as they spill out from beneath the raised longhouse. Then the slight figure of an old man, tattooed and smiling, emerges onto the verandah above. As we don't know a word of the Iban language, we hesitantly try a Malay greeting. 'Selamat Pagi (Good Morning).' He carries on smiling, but a voice answers in English from behind him. It belongs to a confident young Iban boy in a tee shirt and jeans.

The old man beckons, and we mount the ladder and join the communal group of family members sitting on the floor of the long central gallery. We distribute the balloons and pens we have brought for the children and tell the family of our planned walk, via the young interpreter. An hour or so later we leave, accompanied by our new friend who wishes to practise his English and has many questions to ask; he will come with us for part of our walk into Sarawak.

For the first hour or so we chat and walk along a dirt path that leads us deeper into the jungle. The Iban boy, dressed in modern clothing, knows a lot about the plants we pass and their medicinal uses. He keeps a foot firmly in both worlds. In contrast, we only have our feet in the modern one, as we demonstrate when we reach the swamp. It's a bog, swarming with biting insect life, attracted by the dank smell of rotting vegetation. Stretching across it is a line of felled trunks. We have reached the log walk.

Our friend hops nimbly onto the first and leads the way, still talking and shooting questions at us. We follow, and the logs begin to behave like rolling pins at a marathon bake-off. I try holding out my arms for balance but, promptly, fall off into the knee-deep warm water surrounding us. The next few hours are a physical and mental test. My fellow teacher has the idea of using branches as poles to steady ourselves, but even with these, we make slow progress, much to our new friend's amusement. I suspect he regularly enjoys this spectacle. All my concentration is needed just to stay upright and inch my way forward. Presented with the log challenge, I behave like my house geckos encountering the unfamiliar obstacle of a ceiling fan or fridge.

We have stopped to take a rest when several Iban people come into view on the logs ahead. They are smiling and carrying large items on their heads as they trot casually along the logs towards us. Stunned into silence, we stand aside in the swampy water as a complete suite of rattan furniture, sofa, armchairs and dining table, passes by. It is like a moving conveyor belt of prizes on a television game show.

'Terima kasih (Thank you),' they grin at us and greet our young friend. He's a relative, it seems. Having tired of the show of clumsy tumbling foreigners, he decides to turn back for home with his cousins. With a parting smile he wishes us a good walk.

It is dark when we reach Marudi on the Baram River and, certainly, more than six hours since we started our walk. Our legs no longer feel like our own. We find a small bar offering food and free karaoke. After a cold beer and a plate of fried noodles, but eschewing the karaoke, we book into a guest house and fall asleep, to dream about rolling logs.

We return to Brunei the next day, by the same route, taking more time to notice the exotic plant life on the way back. Tall gingers with striking red and yellow flowers are an unexpected sight on the forest floor, while back in the swamp, we stumble along the log walk again, faring no better but knowing that firmer ground lies ahead.

As we draw near to Labi again, something flies across my path to land on a nearby tree. Flattened against the trunk, I can see it is a small lizard. Its ribcage is expanded, like a parachute in preparation for lift-off. I recognise it as a flying tree gecko. Its red mouth gapes and head nods aggressively in my direction. Suddenly, it launches itself into the air again, gliding gracefully to the next tree. I think of my own house geckos, less agile and still learning to negotiate the unfamiliar hazards of the human environment they have moved into. As I have learned, in this new-old world of contradictions it is all too easy to put a foot wrong!

See Borneo and East Malaysia map on page 242.

A Hitchhiker's Guide
to the Bay of Biscay

The continental ferry bobbed about, large though it was, like a geographically challenged rubber duck. We were crossing the Bay of Biscay, heading towards the north coast of Spain—in a haphazard sort of way. Our ship was three hours behind schedule. The emergency evacuation of a sick passenger had taken it off course and towards France so that a helicopter could reach us. Now the tail end of Storm Lorenzo was whipping us on towards our intended destination.

Up on deck ten, our small group of whale watchers huddled together, swaying slowly in unison with the vessel. We might have been football supporters performing a Mexican wave but for our waterproofs and the binoculars pressed firmly to our faces as we scoured the sea around us. We were here for a purpose: volunteering our time to survey whales near the continental shelf where the Atlantic Ocean plummets unimaginable fathoms into deep dark canyons below. Down there the whales fed, occasionally surfacing to fill their giant lungs with air before plunging down again. We had made a few sightings, a blow of white spray or forceful waterspout in the distance. But the creatures themselves had been harder to see and identify. When they broke surface unruly whipped-up waves, white and frothy, shielded their backs and dorsal fins from our probing eyes.

'Coming for a coffee?' my cabin mate asked, clasping binoculars in hands blotchy with cold, as her black beanie hat dripped rainwater onto the deck between us. 'I'll join you in a bit,' I answered. I was still hankering after something more. She left.

Turning back to the sea, with elbows propped on the ship's rail, I raised my binoculars again, gradually becoming mesmerised by the slate-grey waves, unceasing and unstill. Half an hour passed before I eventually closed my aching eyes and looked away. The image of the churning seascape stayed with me as I refocussed on my companions. Only three of us remained now. The warm coffee lounge had lured the rest of the group inside. Above us, a lumpy grey blanket of cloud lay untidily across much of the sky. But the rain had finally stopped and a small corner of the blanket was turned down like a bed ready to climb into. A blue triangle was visible. I watched as the opening grew bigger and a stream of sunlight forced its way through to dance across the sea surface. The waves became calmer and settled into a gentler rhythm, while, around me, patches of dry deck began to appear. I exchanged a gratified smile with my fellow whale watchers.

Suddenly, a shout rang out and a hand pointed energetically. Not at the sea, but behind us, towards the deck on the port side of the ship. At first I could see nothing but the drying deck in front of me. Then a very small dark object entered my field of vision. It was moving erratically through the air. Drawing nearer, I could see a tiny torpedo-like body jerkily moving over the deck towards us and emitting a strange buzzing noise as its wings beat rapidly. My mind jumped back and forth without conviction. Not a bird? A bee then? No. Maybe a hummingbird? Not quite.

'Hummingbird hawk moth,' my neighbour, an expert entomologist, informed me with some satisfaction. 'Autumn migrant. Could be making for Spain or even North Africa.' A migrant. So this unlikely insect, a miniature Cuban cigar with wings, was making the long and hazardous journey to a warmer clime. Earlier in the year thousands of its kind had made their way in the opposite direction to spend their summer sucking up nectar from buddleia and honeysuckle in English gardens. Their rapid wingbeat, with its audible hum, enabled them to hover in mid-air as they probed flowers with their long proboscis.

Our ship must have been a welcome stopover for this fellow traveller and might have brought it closer to its destination. Transfixed, I watched as our enterprising hitchhiker veered away, still humming loudly, and came down to rest somewhere on the stern of the vessel. But it was not alone. From then on we were visited by a stream of other creatures in transit, all hitching a ride as we made our way across the Bay of Biscay. A short-eared owl accompanied us for several hours, sometimes scrutinising other passengers severely as it perched on the railing or circled, observing us from above. Also making the long migration south was a convoy of small birds. The excited twitchers on deck called them out by name as they flew in: chiffchaff, wheatear, meadow pipit, a robin, even a tiny goldcrest—all on the move southwards. The deck became quite crowded with avian guests as they competed for landing space and a quiet corner in which to have a quick preen, freshen up and regain strength.

I didn't see the hummingbird hawk moth again. After resting a while, it must have resumed its journey. Soon a dark line appeared on the horizon, signalling land, and ahead of us a straggle of Spanish fishing vessels could be seen, making their way slowly back to port with the night's catch. I had a hunch I knew where our hitchhiker might be heading to pick up its next ride.

See Spain and Canary Islands map on page 238.

Travels in the Company of P38

Lockdown time produces some strange compulsions. Rummaging through a kitchen drawer, I have unearthed a small metal tool. As I hold it between my fingers, an old memory sheds its cloak of cobwebs and resurfaces for inspection. The object is nearly forty years old now and showing signs of corrosion from much use. It has a personal history, which I will shortly explain. It's flat, rectangular and about three centimetres in length. A small round eyelet has been punched out of one end so that it can be attached to a piece of string or a keyring. This was a useful afterthought of the designer, as it is a small item that could easily be lost. It has an edge shaped into a wave-like curve ending in a pointed lip. Another side is bent into the form of a triangular cutter, which can be quite lethal if you inadvertently get your finger in the way while operating it. I know this to my cost. There is some writing engraved on it—three lines of Hebrew characters. I don't know what they mean, but they probably say something like multi-purpose opener. For that is what the object is, and it has served me to open many a soft drink bottle, can of tuna or jar of preserves while travelling. For some reason, it is known as a P38[2].

---

2   *While writing this I researched my P38 to find out how it got its name. It seems that it was originally developed in the 1940s in the USA and*

It came into my possession in 1984, and after that we became inseparable travelling companions. I was taking some time out, what would nowadays be called a 'gap year', and was working for my keep, rotating between the communal laundry and kitchen, the cotton field and the plastics factory of a kibbutz on the coast of Israel. Appropriately called Nahsholim (The Waves), I had selected it by stabbing a finger on a map in the Kibbutz Volunteering Office a few days after my arrival in Tel Aviv. Nahsholim sat on the silky sands of the Mediterranean, like a child playing in the warm shallow waters of a long curving stretch of azure sea, protected inland by the maternal gaze of Mount Carmel.

After scrubbing tomatoes free of herbicide in the kibbutz kitchen or endlessly ironing shirts in the laundry, I would take a long idyllic walk along the beach, stopping occasionally to examine some curious nobbly orange lumps that protruded from the white sand. I puzzled over them for a long time before realising that they were the sea-tumbled fragments of terracotta amphorae, worn smooth by the waves of centuries and cast up on the shore. Each was once a joint piece, the place where a handle met an elegant neck or the curvaceous body of a Greco-Roman urn. The thumb prints where the Roman potter had pressed them on were still visible. After a lifetime spent transporting olives, wine or oil between the ancient Mediterranean ports, they lay broken and dormant in one of the many wrecks lying on the

supplied to soldiers with their field rations. The story goes that it could open a can faster than its namesake, the P-38 Lightning fighter plane, could fly.

seabed just offshore, before washing up to their final resting place on the beach of Nahsholim.

Sometimes my afternoon walks and archaeological musings were shattered by the deafening noise overhead of an Israeli jet ripping a hole in the sky, as it flew north towards Lebanon on a practice exercise or maybe a military mission. I never knew which and, back then, my untroubled younger self chose not to dwell on this. I also preferred not to reflect too much on the role of the plastic military parts produced by the injection moulding machines that we volunteers operated in the factory. But I should return to the story of my P38.

Towards the end of my stay in Israel, wanderlust gripped me again and I bought a return bus ticket to Egypt. Asking in the kibbutz kitchen for some provisions for the journey, I was given some tins of tuna fish and a stack of pitta bread. I considered the tins for a moment during which the cook must have read my mind. She handed me a P38 and so began our first trip together.

The long meandering coastal road took us westwards, past flat and fertile plains of citrus fruit and avocado. Then our bus swept into the Gaza strip, claustrophobically cramped and poverty-stricken but unenclosed, in those days. Out again and into the Sinai Peninsula, passing between the sweeping expanse of desert on one side and the intense blue seascape on the other. Every few hours we made a rest stop, and I would take out some pitta bread and apply my handy little opener to a can of tuna.

Eventually, a thin ribbon of light appeared far ahead of us, lying across the road and glittering in the sun. The silhouette of a ship moved silently down it and into the desert. A mirage? For a moment I was disoriented by this strange apparition. Then we were crossing it—the Suez Canal. To celebrate, I tore off more pitta bread and reached for my P38 and another tin of tuna. Onwards to Cairo.

In the weeks that followed, together, we travelled 600 or so kilometres down the Nile, taking in all the must-see places of Egypt; first, the pyramids at Giza, and then the temples of Karnak and Luxor. At Luxor I crossed the river and, hiring a bicycle in a moment of madness, I rode out in the noonday sun to the Valley of the Kings. Next stop was the Temple of Isis, a further 200 kilometres downstream. A boat took us out to the island where it now stands, after being dismantled and moved to escape submersion during the building of the Aswan Dam. At this point, the road south ended for us. Inland, the desert beckoned, so we turned towards it and hopped from one oasis settlement to another with the help of a succession of lifts from local truck drivers all the way back to Cairo. I recall the long desert drive with one of them in particular. He had a Demis Roussos cassette tape from the 1970s, which he played continuously as we bounced our way across the sand. Even today, many years later, I cannot think of desert landscapes without the strains of Roussos's love song 'Forever and Ever' flooding my ears.

Along our circuitous route, I restocked with more canned tuna from small Egyptian stores, and my trusty metal companion dangled from its string on my backpack, always at the ready to slit and disembowel their contents, or to flip off the caps from bottles of the local Sprite. This was usually warm and flat but became my choice of thirst quencher in the hot afternoon sun. Eventually my Egyptian adventure and 'time out' in Israel came to an end. Reluctantly, I returned home to look for work, with P38 still optimistically swinging from my pack, perhaps in anticipation of our next trip together.

Now, so many years later, as I turn it over in my hand and notice those Hebrew characters again, I hesitate. To throw it into the charity bag or keep it? I take a tea towel and attempt to restore its shine then replace it gently in the kitchen drawer. After all, its travelling days, like mine, are not necessarily over yet.

See Greece, Crete, Turkey, Egypt and Israel map on page 243.

Rights of Passage

We hear the patrol boat before we see it. A motoric throb resonates from deep within the sea mist. White swirls wrap the dark-pitted peaks of Morocco as they float upwards, mysterious and intangible in the distance.

Their presence reaches out to us, fourteen kilometres away, where we sit on a Spanish beach, scanning the sky with binoculars for specks—specks that could turn out to be honey buzzards, rare black storks or multi-coloured bee-eaters—of any bird of passage with wings of courage to make the short dash over the stomach-churning straits between Europe and Africa in search of a warmer winter on another continent.

Atlantic meets Mediterranean here; one, grey-wild and frothy, the other, blue and volatile. But high above the clashing seas, no birds are making the crossing today. The giant fin whales also eluded us on our boat trip yesterday. No spurting blows or surface-lying logs eyeing us curiously. Those juggernauts of the sea had passed silently through the deep trench beneath us.

Only the high-spirited dolphins tumbled around our dancing boat, their airborne bodies curling in delight as queasy passengers on the deck leaned seawards to part with their breakfast. We were hoping to see more than this.

Instead, this afternoon we hear the patrol boat, see its sleek black body emerge briefly in a mist-free window before it speeds off towards the African coast. Then more sound—the slapping of helicopter blades as one dips down out of the sky onto Las Palomas—the Isle of Doves. Barely an island, this rocky outcrop marks the southernmost point of continental Europe.

Yesterday evening, we walked the kilometre-long causeway linking it to Tarifa on the mainland, halting at its padlocked gate. Frustrated, we stood and peered through the bars. Around us on the sea, exuberant kite surfers swooped and raced, the Levante wind whipping them into the air and across the waves in wild ecstatic joy.

Las Palomas was once a military fort, the guidebook said. In recent times, a detention centre for 'illegals'—mostly young African men, washed ashore in collapsed rubber dinghies. Full of hope, they have spilled out onto the sands of a New World.

An air of secrecy hangs over the fort now. A concealed compound lies at its centre—there, we can just make out some low abandoned barrack buildings, visible only with binoculars from the beach. But perhaps they are not altogether abandoned. Earlier, an unmarked white delivery van crossed the causeway and was admitted through the gates. It left soon afterwards, the closing metal clanking heavily behind it.

Now we turn our binoculars on the helicopter, noting its stiff tail and bulbous cockpit eye. Inside, its belly is crammed with shadowy human outlines; impossible to say how many. It descends onto the island, disappearing into the dark heart, blade noise muffled into silence.

We sit, watching, waiting and squeeze the soft white sand between our toes. The waves, dark with seaweed, quietly lap and curl gently towards us.

Suddenly, the sound of the helicopter reverberates across the water once again. Lighter now with its cargo discharged, it rises like an aggravated insect, before disappearing back into the mist.

We put away our binoculars and look back at the sea, troubled, but knowing we can breathe the salty air of freedom enjoyed by migrating birds and boat-shy whales as they journey through their borderless world.

See Spain and Canary Islands map on page 238.

Searching and Finding

A Long Shot

It was George's idea. I was working when he visited so he wandered into the university library to browse the shelves until my return. On the bottom shelf of the botany section a book caught his eye. *Flora Malesiana* had a single due date stamp on the first page showing that it had been checked out once, twenty five years previously. It looked sad and old, with crinkled pages and fading colour plates. In it, George found a reference to *Balanophoraceae*, a tropical plant family with just forty or so species worldwide and recorded in a few isolated locations in Indonesia. I was unimpressed and sensed trouble ahead. 'Balano what?' I asked, with a frown. 'How are we supposed to find something that rare growing up a mountain in South East Asia?'

My objection was squashed and a few months later, finding that plant became the primary motive for our trip to Indonesia. We researched and planned in the manner that we thought we should for a botanical expedition, but it was the pre-internet era, so our resources were limited. They amounted to a return visit to the university library to delve more deeply into *Flora Malesiana* and a re-reading of our off-the-beaten-track guidebook for practical information about how to get there. This would have to do until we arrived in Indonesia.

Some months later in hot and humid Jakarta, the Tourist Information Office proved to be impressively uninformative about *Balanophoraceae*. The two assistants conferred at length in Indonesian before letting us know that they didn't understand what we were talking about. Instead they tried to interest us in a side trip to Bali for 'very nice beach and very good temple.' I was tempted, but George was not to be persuaded. We listened, declined politely and left.

Undeterred, we set out for Bogor in western Java to try our luck at Kebun Raya, the country's most prestigious botanic garden. We were slightly encouraged by the sign at its entrance, boasting of its 'serene and long-standing' status. In a dusty office, the man on duty was sleeping serenely, but, luckily, he was also head of special collections. We woke him and prepared to interrogate.

As it turned out, we probably knew more than he did about *Balanophoraceae*, thanks to the invaluable *Flora Malesiana*. From the illustration we had seen that its appearance could hardly be described as attractive. The text described its colour as typically yellowish brown since it was lacking in chlorophyll, parasitic and with a fungal look about it. It grew to only a few inches in height and had a club-shaped bulb at its head. This was the inflorescence. Its similarity to a stubby phallus was most likely responsible for its sometime reputation as an aphrodisiac.

After some initial confusion over our hand-drawn picture, carefully copied from the book, the special collections man finally grasped what we were looking for and was able to confirm that *Balanophoraceae* had, indeed, been found growing on the forested slopes of Gunung Gede, a volcanic mountain to the west of Bogor. He hadn't seen the plant himself, although, fortunately, he knew what it looked like. He could offer no more information.

The next day, squeezed with fourteen other passengers into the back of a ten-seater bemo, we journeyed on to Cibodas, one of the entry points for hiking up Mount Gede. From there, our guidebook said it would be possible to reach the summit in around ten hours with an overnight break at a shelter, purported to be somewhere on the way. After registering our intention at the small basecamp office—'just to climb the volcano,' we said, in order to keep things simple—we set off along the cobbled path leading up into the forest. There, at the start, it looked like the entry point to a neat, prize-winning village garden. I almost expected to see the trees all bearing Latin labels. They weren't; nevertheless, my confidence increased a little. It might be a long shot, but our plant might just be there, waiting for us. Maybe arrows would even point the way?

There were no arrows; only lush vegetation lined the way. And less than a hundred metres in, the best-kept garden-look totally disappeared. Leaves the size of dinner plates were competing to replace those recently hacked back, and fronds of giant fern hung heavily across the path, threatening to overrun it at any moment. The hungry insect life, which seemed to be emerging from a seven day fast, welcomed us into the rainforest. Towering over us, densely packed trees shielded the sunlight as we stepped deeper inside.

At first, we made frequent forays off the track, scanning around the base of the trees for something resembling that strange little plant that had inspired us. We had little idea of where to look and found nothing resembling our drawing. The muggy air and constant swatting of insects made walking hard work, but every couple of hours we reached a resting point, where the insects took the opportunity of another snack. Often there was a nearby stream from which to refill our water bottles. Rushing ever downwards, their velocity and noise increased the higher we climbed.

More side forays followed, but no *Balanophoraceae*. Where would they grow? Were they even here? The trees wore mossy leggings now and reached out above ground with their twisted roots to trip the unwary. And the cobblestone path had all but disappeared, giving way to hard baked soil. We needed to scramble over decaying tree trunks and bend double to pass under others that had fallen across the path. All were encased in a green carpet, wet velvet to the touch, criss-crossed with sprouting rows of orange toadstools. When we reached out for support, our hands sunk deep into their rotting flanks. As we climbed, we continued our search, but with less and less conviction.

Ahead of us, a waterfall announced itself, and, later, a stream of volcanic hot water that gushed out noisily from a rock face, sending clouds of steam billowing out into the forest. The whole mountain was saturated in water.

Eventually, we reached a tumbledown night shelter. It wasn't inviting. Inside, many of the floorboards had rotted away, but its corroded metal roof was still intact and would protect us from any rain. We unrolled our sleeping bags quietly. We were exhausted from climbing and disappointed not to have found our plant. Darkness fell suddenly and with it a veil of different forest sounds descended. We fell asleep to the relentless rasping of the night-time cicadas.

But the night held a surprise. A scrabbling sound woke us around midnight. It came from the broken floorboards. Frantically, we flashed the torch across the room, expecting to see a large venomous snake swaying towards us. Instead, a pair of small, startled mammalian eyes stared back. A triangular head and spotted torso were poking up out of the floor. They belonged to a weasel-like creature. A palm civet, perhaps, out on a night forage. It surveyed us crossly then turned tail and left.

Morning came and, with it, cooler air, bringing a waft of realism. The scale of the challenge we had set ourselves dawned on us; we were ready to accept defeat gracefully. The final leg up to the summit didn't take long, and we were rewarded with a stunning view over tropical forest from the volcano rim. There, growing at the top, we even found a plant we had not anticipated—a large clump of soft white stars—it was tropical edelweiss. Its felt-fashioned flowers were studded with tiny clinging pearls of dew. We were consoled. It was a good enough substitute for the elusive *Balanophoraceae*.

We began the long descent, intending to make it back to basecamp without stopping, then to hail a ride from a passing bemo back to Cibodas. But, halfway down, we did stop, on an impulse, to take a last peek into the jungly interior beside the path. And there, we found our plant waiting patiently for us. Half hidden by a large tree root, two unmistakeable brown fingers poked rudely up through the soil. A magic moment that caught us by surprise. I still have the photograph to prove it.

See Indonesia map on page 246.

The Dance of the Scorpions

'Alacran!' White teeth light up the face of the Mexican stallholder as he grins and gestures towards his scorpion wares. There, dangling, among colourful ceramic pots and ponchos, are bundles of keyrings. A scorpion is attached to each, interred in a plastic chamber and suspended in the sleep of death.

My gaze wanders, taking in ashtrays, clocks and other scorpion-embellished bric-a-brac. Everywhere I see *Centruriodes suffusus*, the unwilling star of the local souvenir industry. Feigning a smile, I move on. I'm pinning my hopes on seeing a live specimen.

I have read about this scorpion, a native of the dry northern deserts around the city of Durango, but also a migrant here, living secretly side by side with the human residents. It keeps a low profile but has a tough life. Hiding skills don't help much in the face of an army of alacraneros (scorpion hunters), whose own livelihoods depend on collecting it each day.

I leave behind the vibrant colours and sweet vegetable smells of the indoor market, and I am swallowed up in the anarchy of the street. The heat and dust hit me. Dodging the traffic, I slip into the cool interior of the university building, a faded three-storey

affair in Spanish colonial style, and where I am temporarily
sharing an office during my stay.

Up to the second floor in the lift, a bouncy jarring ride,
there is a buzz of excitement as I enter. Surprised, I glance
around. And then a collegial hand offers me a glass container.
I take a step backwards; inside are two scorpions, captive and
agitated.

Somewhere deep within the dry adobe walls of the building,
a wrong turn was taken. A mistake that brought these scorpions
into dangerous human terrain. My Mexican friends have detained
them in the office for my benefit.

I take a closer look and see two yellow-brown bodies, flattened
like Formula One racing cars. Each is armed with a pair of nee-
dle-thin pincers that give a menacing wave to distract attention
from their business end: a tail loaded with a potent pouch of
venom that can effortlessly kill a healthy adult.

'Le gustaría verlos? Ven conmigo por favor.' Jose Miguel, a
technician and the self-appointed scorpion handler, leads me
up to the flat roof and there we gingerly open the jar. Scorpions
tumble onto concrete. Liberated but with no place to hide, they
are uncertain in these new surroundings. Then, recovering, they
begin to move about jerkily as if to an inaudible music. Two silent
flamenco dancers, pincers held high, executing short coordinated
steps; their dance is intense and indignant.

Under the hot Latin American sun, I watch them perform,
mesmerised by synchronised footwork, beckoning pincers and
beguiling curved tails. Abruptly, I feel a wave of remorse. I did

not wish this venue or these circumstances on them, and I fear what the future holds for this species.

'Gracias,' I mumble. My scorpion handler circles at a respectful distance, gently coaxing them back into the jar with a long stick. Later, I learn that an evolutionary quirk is helping in their fight for survival. Interbreeding with a species from nearby Zacatecas, the Durango scorpion has transformed itself into an even more deadly hybrid. There is hope.

Rooftop performance over, I accompany Jose Miguel to release my flamenco stars in the desert, far from human territory. There, they will live to dance another day.

See Mexico and Costa Rica map on page 239.

Tongue-tied in
the Land of Magyars

'Sekesh …' I pause and start again, 'Sekesh…fe…
something.' It's no good. I can't say it. I'm in conversation with the Hungarian woman sitting next to
me on Airbus 320, and she has innocently asked, 'Where is the
conference you go to?' But my tongue has seized and I make
a linguistic goulash of it. Our exchange falters, so I switch to
asking her about Budapest, which is easier to say. The plane will
be landing there shortly.

It's a blustery day in early September 2008 when the aircraft
wheels bump along the runway, and its brake pads announce
our arrival with a squeal. It's my first visit to Hungary, and I
am curious about what I will find. I am on my way to give a
presentation at Kodolanyi Janos University, in a city sixty-four
kilometres southwest of Budapest, with an unpronounceable
name. There is a shorter version of it, but I can't remember that
either. My guidebook tells me it translates as 'white castle'.

My destination is the regional capital of Central Transdan-
ubia, and it lies along the route to Lake Balaton. At least my
time in Budapest will grant me a few days to learn how to say

it before I face the challenge of buying a bus or train ticket for my onward journey.

The next morning, I venture out of my hotel and into central Budapest for a first taste of Hungary. Standing outside Saint Stephen's Basilica, I am halfway down page twenty-three of my guidebook, reading about its historical background, when I hear a deep male voice behind me speaking accented but almost flawless English. It turns out to be Florian, a resourceful university student, who is leading a gaggle of tourists on his own alternative tour of Budapest's unmissable sights.

Drawn by his impeccable command of English, I take a step closer and listen in. He notices me and takes me aside while his small flock debate whether to go inside to visit the Chapel of the Holy Right Arm, containing the mummified forearm of the country's patron Saint István, as Stephen is called, or to continue inspecting the neo-classical features of the external architecture. Explaining that he funds his studies partly by giving walking tours, Florian invites me to join them and make a voluntary donation at the end, if I wish. I accept and attach myself to the group.

The next stop on the Florian tour is a small inconspicuous square, meditating quietly a short distance from the sun-speckled girth of the river Danube, which separates Buda from Pest. On one side of the square stands a faded theatre, where the young Beethoven once performed; another, is occupied by the imposing building of the Hungarian Academy of Sciences. Our knowledgeable young guide reels off a list of scientific inventions created by his imaginative countrymen: the ballpoint pen—the brainchild of László Bíró; the safety match, binoculars, carbonated water and, of course, the one I knew and grappled with as a teenager, Ernő Rubik's—irritating—cube. These inventions, conceived by the minds of practical Hungarians, became indispensable (or compulsive) accessories to twentieth century life.

I am beginning to get a sense of this proudly independent country, rich in eccentricity and originality. And Budapest is turning out to be an experience full of surprises and delightful discoveries. After another hour or so of secretive squares and back alleyways, we end our tour in front of a student refectory, where Florian has brought us to sample some cheap but authentic Hungarian cuisine of the hearty home-cooked variety.

The canteen cook is a sturdy Mother Hungary figure, with sleeves rolled-up above forearms that are worthy of a gymnast on the parallel bars. Without looking at us, she serves out large helpings of steaming hot goulash laced with paprika. It is the only dish on the menu. Thankfully, today, we are spared the lunchtime challenge of trying to order one of the eye-wateringly long dish names on the menu of a local restaurant. An hour later we leave the refectory with full stomachs and tip Florian generously for his excellent all-round service. He has thought of everything.

Over lunch I have made the acquaintance of another member of Florian's hand-picked flock. Marguerite is Canadian and on a career break from her job as a freelance journalist in Quebec province. She has never been out of Canada before, but in the pioneering spirit of her ancestors has chosen to make a solo tour of Eastern Europe overland, inventing an itinerary as she zigzags from one country to another. She has already ticked off Russia, Poland and the Baltic states and is now working her way around Hungary. I am deeply envious and want to hear more, so, in the afternoon, I tag along with her to the Széchenyi open-air thermal baths.

'Are you going to write a book about your trip?' I ask as we sit neck-deep in the deliciously warm waters under an open blue sky.

'Perhaps,' she replies. I probe further. 'Where are you going after Hungary?' She doesn't know, maybe east to Ukraine or south towards the border with Romania. I am fascinated by her undertaking, which smacks of adventure.

Then she turns the tables. 'And what about you? Where are you going after Budapest—for your conference?' I fail to rise to the occasion, 'It's a place called Sekesfe … something.' Tapping my forehead in exasperation, I search for an excuse, 'It has a long name with too many consonants. I can't seem to fix it in my memory.'

I look around for an escape from my embarrassment. We are surrounded by Budapestians at play, frolicking like a raft of otters in the therapeutic waters. These are the largest medicinal baths in Europe served by two thermal springs, which maintain the pools' temperature in the mid-70 degrees Celsius.

Fun, flirtation and boardgames fill the afternoon for the baths' visitors. Toddlers are receiving their first swimming lessons from watchful parents; teenage couples out on afternoon dates flick water at each other; half-immersed elderly men with spindly arms and flopping stomachs are engrossed in poolside chess matches. They are all here soaking up the healing benefits of the ion-rich thermal waters.

And behind us extends a complex of buttercup-yellow stone terraces and Neo-Baroque-style buildings, which house saunas, steam rooms, changing rooms and lockers. Wrapped in the luxurious heat and stroked by the invisible underwater hands of the waters' warm thermals, Marguerite and I sit and while away the afternoon.

Only as the sun starts to set over the unbroken surface of an almost empty pool do we reluctantly emerge and go our separate ways; Marguerite, to choose between taking a route towards Ukraine or one to Romania; and me, to search for transport to a place with an unpronounceable name.

I settle for road over rail, and the next morning make my way to the bus station. From here, there are buses departing for the city where my conference will be held. Silently, I pass the man in the ticket office a slip of paper with its name written on. He nods. Money exchanges hands and I have my ticket. After that the journey is straightforward.

When I arrive, I have some time before my conference the following day, so I use it to explore my new surroundings. The cobbled streets are full of statues of Saint István, revered King of the Magyars. Here he is sitting bolt upright on a throne with his giant hands resting on his knees; there he is astride a prancing horse. Then I discover that he has a particular connection with this place; the ruins of his Royal Palace are here and his sarcophagus too.

But István is not the only pervasive presence. Other life-size mannequins of a less saintly and more quirky character populate the streets. Outside a wine bar sits a stuffed caricature of a local imbiber in checked shirt and braces, lolling tipsily from a rickety chair. Is he a promotion for the shop's wine stock, perhaps, or a warning against the dangers of excessive drinking? I cannot decide.

As I walk, I need to skirt around an outdoor display of the city's artwork. Bronze figurines are frozen in perpetual promenade on the pavement. One is of a toothless old lady dressed in a headscarf, wheeling a cart and smirking broadly. 'Aunt Kati' as she is called, commemorates a local market-woman who, even in her nineties, continued to sell milk, sour cream and roast duck in these streets. She captures something of the idiosyncratic nature of this country's people. Beside her, in the flour-dusted window of a bakery giant loaves of artisan bread, the size of plumped up cushions, are stacked in an unsteady tower.

Near the end of my exploratory walk in Sekesfe-something, I stop, perplexed, in front of some iron railings. They are covered in rows of hanging padlocks in all shapes and sizes. Is it a graveyard for padlocks? Their final resting place when they become separated from their keys? A small sign bears some words, which I find in my guidebook: Szorelmsek Kerítés. It means a fence for lovers, and they are so-called love locks. Found on bridges, gates and fences throughout Hungary, the locks are put there by couples making a public promise of undying love to each other. I walk away with a niggling concern about the keys. What happens to them, I wonder? Are they destined to a life of separation from their other half? But my time has run out and I need to look over my presentation again before tomorrow.

In the opening address of the conference, I hear the president of our elite little academic gathering stumble over the pronunciation of the name of our host city, which she too has been unable to master. I smirk but then feel a prick of shame and make a decision.

Several days later, when I arrive back at Gatwick airport the passport control officer throws a non-threatening question at me as he scans my document and hands it back. 'Where have you been?'

Finally, I am ready. I wiggle my tongue in a quick warm-up exercise, take a deep breath and mentally count off the five syllables as I confidently produce my answer, 'Székesfehérvár.' With a tinge of pride at my fluency, I enjoy his look of total incomprehension.

See Germany, Czech Republic and Hungary map on page 247.

Where Europe Ends

A forest of squelchy moss lies under our feet. It's unwilling to let us pass and sucks at our boots as we, the walkers, trudge along. Here and there, the heavy raised heads of sunken boulders watch silently. I fear they are mythical Nordic giants buried deep in the earth. Some are crowned with curly wigs of bleached green lichen; others, tattooed with a patchwork of black lines—the aptly named map lichen. We stop walking and sink deeper into this primeval world. It's still drizzling as we pore over our own map, which is already soggy despite its plastic sleeve. I shake the cold compass back to life. We study the map, confer and make a sixty-degree turn to the left. It's that way…we think.

We are in the far north of Norway, midnight sun territory, high above the Arctic Circle, and we have been lost for some hours, perhaps, stumbling around in circles. The northernmost end of continental Europe is not far from here. But which way? This peninsula is called Knivskjellodden—it's a finger of land pointing prophetically out across the wild North Sea towards the North Pole, 2000 or so kilometres away. Its fingertip is actually one and a half kilometres further north than North Cape, the tourist destination, which we have scornfully turned our backs on. The coastal E69 route ends there, but we have stopped a few kilometres short and parked our car on the roadside; to reach our goal, we have ten more, of watery tundra to walk through and no path.

It's a mystical landscape, bathed in the eerie twilight of a sun that never dips below the horizon at this time of year, and we are not alone here. Without the security of trees, small birds roosting in the boulder crevices flit out, up and away, when disturbed by our footfall. Signs of larger creatures litter the moss around us too: antlers, the discarded headgear of reindeer after the rutting season. Some have lain here for months and gleam bone-white in their mossy beds. Others shed more recently, still bear, tattered red ribbons of velvet reindeer skin, slowly being eaten away in the rain. Their previous owners are growing new ones now, as they wander their summer grazing grounds on the coast.

A curtain of mist has dropped all around. We walk on with tired feet and ebbing confidence. We were supposed to inform the police if we ventured across the tundra, but we didn't. Presumably, others, with a thirst for adventure, have also lost their way here. Too late now. We struggle on. Ahead of us, the mist stirs and parts. An apparition moves out of it. Then another. Shadowy alien shapes slowly materialise into… a herd of reindeer! A straggly line of animals that stops in surprise at the sight of two trespassers in their kingdom. They gaze at us and the silence of the moment is everlasting. A muffled snort breaks the spell, and, losing interest, they turn away and resume their foraging.

I try to ignore the dampness that has seeped through my jacket and turned my skin cold. Instead, I concentrate on the ground as I walk, focusing on the tapestry of small plants: red, yellow, brown and green, all clinging to life in this impoverished and saturated soil. More time passes. The small hours have descended, but the light persists in this strange, sleepless place. We are walking uphill now—to the sea? This can't be right. But it's just a small ridge, which we pass over. And then! We hear it first, quite unexpectedly, and music to our ears: the sound of waves tumbling the pebbles on the shore.

We have reached our journey's end. From this ridge above the tideline, we sigh in relief and look out, surveying the foamy water as it breaks on the beach below.

Here at the end of the world, the shore is strewn with flotsam and jetsam. Plant debris has floated in from distant lands, borne on the boisterous waves; other items have been flung off cargo ships in rough seas, as they've navigated the shipping lane around the top of Norway: bits of broken crates with indecipherable markings denoting exotic countries of origin, and a jigsaw of unrecognisable twentieth century plastic, water-stressed and reduced to fragments, doomed to last forever. But, it is a beach-comber's paradise. We gladly drop our packs, tent and sleeping bags onto the pebbles, flex our weary shoulders and claim our reward, wandering beside the water and gently turning over the shore's treasures with our feet to examine them.

Later, I am standing on an exposed black rock that juts out into the sea. I look towards where the North Pole must surely lie. The wind pummels the hood of my jacket, and, deep inside, my ears hear these sounds as muffled explosions, drowning out the roar of the ocean. I congratulate myself—from this vantage point I can draw a line between me and the North Pole with nothing in between. We made it to the end of Europe.

Then, something just offshore disturbs the water. The slick and sliding surface parts, and a dark mottled head, sleek and whiskery, rises from the depths. The Roman nose of a grey seal, its nostrils open, and a pair of alert marble eyes, dark and shiny, regard me curiously as I stare back. My imaginary line has been breached, but now I will always remember this moment. The seal sinks back into the crow-black depths.

It's very late and we are spent. Further up the beach, we unpack and pitch the tent badly, unroll damp sleeping bags and crawl inside for a few hours' sleep. Tomorrow, that is later today, we must find our way back[3].

See Sweden, Norway, Finland and Russia map on page 248.

---

3   *This walk took place in 1997. There is now a marked trail and well-trodden footpath leading across the tundra to the northernmost point of Europe at the end of the Knivskjellodden peninsula.*

Displaced on the Spanish Plain

This morning, I am leaving the hotel with a headful of television images. Over breakfast, I learned that Catalonia is declaring independence from Spain. The plazas are crowded in Barcelona and Madrid with scenes resembling surging whirlpools, protesters for independence or for national unity. Randomly, eruptions of mayhem flash across the screen. Convoluted legal debates were taking place in the television studio. But the arguments confused me, an outsider, travelling in an unfamiliar land. Outside the hotel I pause and re-orientate myself then set off towards the Estación de Tren de Salamanca. Perhaps a day inside the medieval walls of Avila will offer some relief from a troubled present.

We leave precisely on time. The October sky is clear blue. Fields, stubbled with gold, stretch far across the plain, melting invisibly into the distant sierra. High up, a ropey formation of griffon vultures effortlessly rides a warm thermal, searching for carrion below. The train from Salamanca is almost empty and carries me eastwards. Avila was the home of Teresa: saint, mystic and, according to my guidebook, a discalced Carmelite nun. Dis-calced. The fields drift by outside as I crack the word in two like an egg, looking for meaning inside.

I delve back into my guidebook, the 1500s and Teresa of Avila, living here on the Spanish plain. And discalced? I turn a page. Here it is—'without shoes.' Hers was a strict religious order; the nuns went barefoot.

For a while, I read on about this woman of visions and ecstatic trances, living out her life of austerity and contemplation in difficult times. Then the gentle rocking of the train lulls me into sleepiness. I lean against the window and let the plain and sky wash over me until the train coasts gently into Avila station.

A straight road leads to the old walled town ending at its imposing eleventh century gateway. Somewhere inside is a convent, built over her birthplace. But first, I meet an unexpected maze of cobbled streets. I am not alone here. Other visitors have arrived ahead of me, and long pilgrim processions, as well as confusing signposts, bar my way.

I drift around, helplessly lost for a time. When the museum dedicated to her life and work reveals itself the door is closed. In the nearby gift shop the man at the counter just shrugs, unable or unwilling to explain when it might reopen.

I wander away and, by chance, arrive at another highlight on the Teresa tour: the Monasterio de la Encarnación, open and displaying the monastic cell where she lived for forty years. The nun in charge leads me to a wooden door, which she opens with an outsized iron key. She demonstrates the bell pulley for calling to be let out. Then I am alone, feeling slightly disconcerted and enclosed in a room full of curious personal effects, in ageing glass cabinets. I approach one of them: parchment scraps, covered in a faded cryptic writing of enigmatic loops and curls. I see Teresa relics—the ossified ring finger of her right hand, a walking stick, a flagellation rope. My eyes wander restlessly. I notice a small cell in the corner of the room, a stone wall and a hard chair.

I inspect the contents of more cabinets, curious but feeling like an intruder. Our lives are centuries apart. It's hard to find connections. I take a step towards the bell pulley, then stop. Lying among the relics is a loop of misshapen brown beads—no, they are not real beads but acorns. It must be a prayer rosary. A homemade one, her own. Local acorns, collected after an autumn fall, and threaded together. After a lifetime of use they are worn smooth by handling and darkly weathered. I am somehow touched by this. A deeply personal possession; it has survived the turmoil of the centuries and now quietly bides its time here.

Later, on the train back to Salamanca, a scene drifts before my mind's eye: a woman, barefoot, sitting on a hard chair, fingers methodically working dry acorns. She's praying in silence and crossing the threshold into an ineffable elsewhere. Taking a step into eternity.

My vision is broken by the sound of the guard passing through. The passenger opposite me is reading a newspaper; its front page displays turbulent scenes in the Spanish capital. I am thrust back into the uneasy present. Teresa said, 'Life is like a night in a bad hotel.' Her world or mine? Outside, the fields slip by endlessly as the plain unravels, marked only by a solitary oak tree.

See Spain and Canary Islands map on page 238.

The Lure of a Landscape

A mauve taxi, scratched and dusty, pulls up outside the hotel where we stand waiting. Out of the window leans the driver. 'Presa Francisco Zarco?' I enquire. He nods and we get in. For an agreed fare, my university colleague and I are taking a ride out to a dam in the semi-arid Mexican desert.

The three-day conference I have come to Durango state to attend has ended; my presentation has been given, the networking sessions are over, and the much-anticipated conference dinner has been eaten. Most of the delegates have gone home, and only a few throw-away coffee cups litter the tables in the conference hall. But we are staying on, and we have twenty-four hours in which to relax before our week-long workshops begin. So, this bright and balmy day in late January offers an opportunity to see what lies beyond Victoria de Durango, the state capital.

Admittedly, a visit to a dam and lakeside picnic spot in the semi-barren hills of Mexico was not part of my original agenda. Yesterday, in the tourist information office I struggled to explain, in halting Spanish, that I wanted to go to la Zona del Silencio, the so-called Silent Zone—a large empty chunk of dry desert landscape, reputed to be so 'dead' that it is impenetrable to radio transmissions, although apparently visited by extra-terrestrials quite regularly. The zone stretches into the northern part of Durango state, and, when I discovered this, I had an urge to visit it.

My urge had a literary source—a book about cacti to be precise, bought in a moment of excited anticipation, soon after learning that I would be presenting my 2007 paper on technology-assisted language learning at a conference in Mexico, the cactus capital of the world. Among the host of endemic plants and animals found in the desert landscape, I was thrilled to learn that the rare purple nopales cactus had been recorded right there in the Silent Zone.

The door to my imagination opened and realism fled out through the window. Could I track down this celebrity of the Mexican cactus A-list? If not during a coffee break between conference sessions, then surely afterwards. First, I would need to visit the tourist office to find out how to get there. So I did.

When I finally manage to bridge the communication gap with the girl fronting the information desk, she is apologetic, explaining that there are no tours of the Silent Zone at this time of year: 'No es la temporada, Senora.'

But I badly want to walk in the Mexican desert and find this rare cactus. She sees my disappointment and has a solution, of sorts. A taxi is booked for a day excursion to the Francisco Zarco dam, a few hours' drive away. The driver will come to our hotel the following morning. I accept this consolation prize gracefully, persuade my bemused conference colleague to come along, and the Silent Zone drops quietly off my Mexican agenda.

The drive out along a stretch of Federal Highway 40, linking Durango and Mazatlán, follows a curvaceous route through the foothills of the Sierra Madre Oriental, a range of mountains extending down the eastern flank of northern Mexico, and running parallel to its sister range, the Sierra Madre Occidental, on the pacific side of the country. From time to time, we pass over a bridge spanning a deep canyon, and the views are impressive.

The grey-brown topography here resembles a rumpled apron gathered into hilly ruches and pleats and studded with clumps of xerophytic plants and a few stunted trees. There are also cacti among them, but, sadly, I see no flashes of purple.

'Do you know who Francisco Zarco was?' my colleague asks. I turn away from the taxi window. I don't, but our guidebook apparently does. The man honoured with his very own dam turns out to have been a nineteenth century journalist from Durango who then made his name in the high-risk world of Mexican politics.

Some while later, we arrive at the wide reservoir lake, created by Francisco's dam, and our mauve taxi comes to a stop just a metre or two from the shoreline and its gently lapping water. The driver promptly gets out of the car and, from a jacket pocket, produces a packet of Delicados, a cheap brand of Mexican cigarette. He leans against the bonnet of his car, facing the lake vista, and falls into a deep meditation.

The expanse of water is glistening in the soft sunlight, its surface radiating a sense of serenity. A cigarette dangles from between his nicotine-stained fingers, emitting a thin straggle of smoke slowly upwards through the dry air. This picture could rival that of the famous Marlboro cowboy who advertised the other tobacco brand that is smoked in Mexico.

We leave the scene and turn inland, walking across the stony ground towards a different outlook. A depleted landscape. But the almost barren hillside reaches out to us in a warm and welcoming hug. It is a landscape for solitude and rumination, predisposed to turn visitors inwards and so we drift apart and explore our separate ways.

I wander off towards some small patches of vegetation. Here and there is a cactus, asleep in the stony spot where it has grown for decades, waiting patiently to be discovered. A barrel cactus sits, half buried in soil, with only its crown poking out in a severe crew cut. Another spiney specimen stands like a boxed-in candelabra, its arms thrust upwards as if to claim the blue sky above for itself. Other cacti strike out horizontally—endowed with a mass of woolly sausage-like arms that clamber over each other as they feel their way into new terrain. A hotch-potch of curiously formed drought-tolerant specimens that resolutely adhere to a harsh landscape.

There is one that I recognise, and it's a member of the nopales tribe, although, regretfully, not the purple one. It's a close cousin of the prickly pear, now found all over Mediterranean Europe. Mexico boosts over one hundred nopales species, and they are hard to tell apart, unless they are purple, of course. The one in front of me strikes a comical pose for my camera, with its flat grey paddle-shaped arms stretching out on different planes, as if ready for a frenetic game of multi-armed table tennis.

I wonder if this one might be the species that has found its way into many Mexican dishes. During the conference a fellow delegate invited me to share her lunch, a takeaway Durango-style.

'What are they?' I asked, unable to tell my enchiladas from my tacos. But they were neither.

'Gorditas,' she replied. 'Gorditas de nopales. It means little fat ones in English.' It was a good name to describe the round pouches stuffed to bursting with spiced cactus flesh. After that, nopales cropped up everywhere in Mexican cuisine: served with eggs—huevos con nopales, and with meat—carne con nopales; then sliced and raw as a side salad or juiced in jugo de nopales.

A flitting movement interrupts my gastronomic musing. It's a bird darting from its lookout point on one cactus to the top of another: a woodpecker of some kind—with a coffee-coloured chest and head, and black and white checked wings. It has a red spot on its crown, and it is clearly agitated by my proximity. As it swoops in front of me again, I follow it with my eyes, and then look back. The tall cactus it has just flown from has a gaping wound in its side, halfway up the main stem: a round hole with edges collapsing inwards and with a few bits of dry grass poking out.

Abruptly, like a cuckoo clock, a head pops out of the hole to assess the disturbance. The woodpecker's mate has been sitting inside on a nest, which has been built after first drilling out a chunk of the hard green flesh. There are very few trees here, but a tall cactus will do as an alternative home. Seeing me, she too flies off, and I am left to admire this piece of woodpecker handiwork.

The faint sound of a voice echoes from the hillside above. My name is being called. It is my colleague hailing me. She points towards the parked car. It is time to head back to the city and prepare for our workshops. We stumble back down. Although a good hour has passed, the driver is exactly as we left him, propped against the front of his car, cigarette in hand, his gaze lost in the distant view of hills. A scattering of extinguished cigarette stubs lies in the dust at his feet, forming a miniature map, like the cacti stamped onto the desert landscape.

In the taxi back, my colleague and I swap stories about our discoveries. I tell her about the woodpeckers nesting in the cactus and pull out a little book I have been given by the conference organiser: *A Guide to the Birds of Durango* by Bishop and Santiesteban, two local ornithologists. Inside, I find a picture resembling the bird I saw: a Gila woodpecker, a species known for excavating nest holes in cacti. I show it to my colleague.

'No purple cactus then?' she asks, recalling my earlier obsession.

No. But we agree that it's been a good day spent in the peace and tranquillity of the semi-desert, on a hillside above a lake, looking at the landscape with new eyes. Not so barren after all, it has shared some of its secrets with us, and I am satisfied. This time, we'll leave the Silent Zone to the extra-terrestrials, who might even discover some purple nopales there; if they're lucky.

See Mexico and Costa Rica map on page 239.

A Chance Occurrence

The Arrival

'The time is perfect,' the boy in the matching olive-green shirt and shorts tells us, as he pushes the key to our cabaña across the reception desk. With his other hand, he picks up the wad of Costa Rican colones we have just put down.

We look at him blankly. He continues, 'For the arribada, no? Maybe tonight or after tonight.' An arrival? Who? A visiting dignitary, perhaps? A government minister or film star? It sounded interesting. But we are in a hurry to take our first shower in several days, so we thank him, take our key and enquire no further.

We have made the long drive from the capital, San José, to the Parque Nacional Santa Rosa, on the Pacific coast of Costa Rica, in our hire car, a small blue jeep that we have nicknamed Hotel Feroza, as it also serves as our mobile home from time to time—a mosquito-proof metal box to sleep in when the plagues of biting insects, that descend nightly on the outdoor camping sites, become too much to bear. But tonight there will be the luxury of a cabaña, with soft beds and a private shower, before we explore the park tomorrow.

There are only a handful of other visitors at the moment, and they all look similar to ourselves: foreign tourists, mostly on the trail of Costa Rican wildlife and here to explore some tropical dry forest. As we walk towards our cabaña, we notice the chattering birdlife in the surrounding forest. There is a sense of anticipation in the air. It is not yet high season, but, despite the dearth of visitors, it is not entirely quiet. In the cafeteria, when we stop by to check out the menu, there is also an irrepressible bubbling sense of excitement. From a seated group of park staff hoots of laughter erupt like sporadic gas emissions belching out of a volcanic mud pool. It's not clear why.

'You come for arribada?' After the third time of being asked by a park ranger, we give in and answer as expected of us, 'Yes, okay. But who is coming and where and when?' The response confuses us. The arrival is certainly imminent, and, if we are lucky, we will witness it. So, what is going to happen? It seems that there will be no famous visitor, but in that case we haven't quite grasped what it's all about.

We must go to Playa Naranjo, we are told, a beach some thirty kilometres away. And we need to leave soon to arrive there by this evening. There is little time to lose. So, the shower is put on hold, and we take up our backpacks again.

Once we have left the park headquarters, the first part of the walking trail to the beach takes us through a long stretch of savannah grassland, a jagged yellow scar in the forest landscape that is evidence of a previous slash and burn culture. A cloud of scorching dry air hangs overhead. It is disinclined to budge. We make our way through the savannah. Despite a copious amount of sun protection cream, my skin is tingling from the fierce sun. I squint and see that we are walking towards a distant line of shimmering trees, the edge of the forest.

We leave the open oven of the savannah and enter the forest where the cooler shade comes as instant relief. We are not alone here. A troupe of pumped-up howler monkeys has seen us arrive. We heard their deep-throated roaring from the savannah and knew they were somewhere nearby. They give us a hostile reception. Peering down at us through the leafy canopy, they shake the branches and shriek simian profanities, then pelt us with branches and leaves as we pass below them. Their message is clear—we are unwelcome visitors.

We walk quickly through their territory into that belonging to a family of peccaries, grubbing for roots in the leaf litter. We hear their scuffling and porcine snorts of indignation as their barrel bodies barge clumsily away into deeper undergrowth.

Playa Naranjo is somewhere ahead, but there is still mangrove to pass through before we reach it. Much later we emerge from the trees into this new landscape. The ferocious heat outside the forest hits us again, but the mangrove pools of warm brackish water at least provide a place to soak my tee shirt. I am startled by a psychedelic fleet of blue and red shrimps scooting out to investigate this white floating apparition breaking the surface of their pool. When I pull it back on, I feel my body temperature fall a delicious degree or two.

Watchful crabs lurk behind mangrove roots, each brandishing a mighty claw of false bravado but ready to dash to its burrow at the slightest movement. I am thinking about the cabina and shower we had promised ourselves when we get our first sight of the Pacific Ocean and hear its volatile surf crashing up onto the sand.

This is the place where we have been told to come. We find an area at the back of the beach designated as a campsite, but it is deserted. There will be few witnesses of the event, if it happens. But farther around the curve of the bay, two figures are squatting in the sand, watching the ocean and a solitary brown pelican idly floating beyond the breaking surf.

We find some shade and rest, drinking water and nibbling dry biscuits slowly to pass the time, content to wait. It is about five o'clock when the light starts to dim. The sun sets quickly here. Brushing the tickling sand from our legs, we pile our packs in a heap and wander at the water's edge. The two figures and the pelican are gone now. The sea is calmer and almost expectant, the lapping of the waves reduced to a quiet murmur. Tonight there will be a new moon. We walk halfway around the bay before we notice a low domed rock just where the water is ebbing away from the shore. It is smooth and dark in the dwindling light. We will turn there.

We draw closer but there is no rock. The dome is moving, laboriously heaving itself up the sand, with flippers. It is a sea turtle. A dark green alien reptile sliding out of the sea leaving train tracks behind it. An Olive Ridley, one of the smallest of the seven marine species of turtle, and a female, returning to her natal beach. The place where she first entered the water as a flapping and agitated hatchling some fifteen or more years previously, and which she might call home, despite her oceanic wanderings.

She has travelled thousands of miles across the open ocean from distant feeding grounds to find this exact beach again. Behind her, lingering in the blue depths offshore, are many more of her kind, an invasion fleet waiting to follow. They have mated there, and females in their thousands will emerge from the sea together, arriving over one or two nights to lay their eggs in sandy holes, and then mysteriously disappear from whence they came, not to return for another three years or more. This is their anticipated arribada; an arrival by sea in tens of thousands.

Beyond the turtle's domed shell, farther along the beach, is another one, and behind that another and another, emerging from the foam. A dark straggling line of smaller and smaller humps stretches out for the entire length of the waterline. It is a race, in extreme slow motion, as each creature drags her heavy carapace, then rests and sighs, dark eyes seeping viscous tears to remove the irritating sand.

We squat down behind one female that has found the right spot for her eggs, watching as dexterous hind flippers excavate, feel, pat and shape a neat round pit in the sand. Then in a trance-like state of concentration, she squeezes out a slither of eggs, two by two, perfect ping-pong balls enclosed in a knotty string of mucus. They fall, soft-shelled and gleaming, until eventually she has expelled them all from her body. Her flippers tenderly backfill the pit, tamping it down, before she hauls herself round towards the sea once more.

And as she turns, we see some magic. A flicker of light in the darkness swells and ripples across the surface of her shell, like fairy lights on a Christmas tree quivering into a cascade of luminescence. It is phosphorescent seaweed that has found a foothold and a home on a turtle's back to travel the seven seas with its host. As we marvel at the sight, it flashes out a mystic message, an announcement to celebrate the imminent arrival of new life.

We don't sleep much that night but continue to watch, as wave upon wave of Olive Ridleys emerge from the sea, returning home to lay their eggs. How can the sea contain so many turtles? How do they find their way here? Do they navigate by the stars, like seafaring human travellers used to? It is a mystery.

The beach is strangely empty when the early morning light sneaks in over the horizon. Only the stragglers, those turtles who arrived last, are left. They are slipping back into the surf to resume their nomadic existence without a backward look at the place they will not see again for a few years. Up in the nesting area beneath the sand lies a new generation of turtles, waiting for their turn to go down to the sea.

See Mexico and Costa Rica map on page 239.

Mischievous Gods and
a Serpentine Tangle

I feel the pitching sensation in my stomach as I dream. Am I still on the boat? Only yesterday my body was lurching back and forth on our small cruise boat, which was being assaulted by waves, unleashed by a playful Poseidon as it fought its way out from the harbour into the Aegean Sea. A bigger jolt shakes me awake, and I realise that it is the bed shaking on the uneven flagstones that has woken me. My heart misses a beat. The movement stops. And I nervously sit up and slide my feet out from under the thin cotton sheet before lowering them onto the cool floor.

Not quite terra firma, but I feel reassured. Just a small earth tremor, I tell myself. I peer at my watch but can't make out the time. The night is hot and dark, but all is still again, so I lie back down and return to my uneasy dreams.

The next morning, when we get up, Helios is already driving his chariot across the sky. As the heat starts to build, we spoon honey into our yogurt at the breakfast table and discuss the tremors of the previous night. A small earthquake of 4.5 with its epicentre somewhere off the Greek coast, the guest house owner has informed us. Far away from the sea, we felt it here in this small town at the foot of Mount Olympus, where we have spent the night on our journey of exploration in this part of the Greek mainland.

And it is, perhaps, not a coincidence that we felt the tremor on the slopes of this mountain. After all, it's the home of Zeus, Greek God Supremo, my companion reminds me. So what was its significance? Was it the rumbling of a discontented deity? Stirring absent-mindedly with a spoon, I watch the swirl of honey descend slowly into the depths of the white whirlpool in my breakfast bowl.

We finish breakfast, and it's time for us to move on. Today we are driving towards the border with Bulgaria. We travel north, passing from Thessaly into Central Macedonia, much later reaching our next destination. It is Lake Kerkini, a large natural reservoir lying in a shallow valley not far from the Greco-Bulgarian frontier. Surrounded by hills and forests, here it may be possible to escape the relentless heat, which has arrived early this year. Hopefully, Greek gods and earthquakes will leave us in peace too.

A long winding road encircles the lake. We pass the next few days making slow laps around it, stopping frequently to observe the wildlife bonanza. When the water level drops in the summer season, great tracts of marshland and wet field are exposed alongside the lake. They teem with all manner of amphibians, reptiles and frantically-feeding water birds.

The first birds that I see and instantly fall in love with are the spoonbills. They are comically exaggerated birds with gangly postures, distinctive spatula bills and white head crests that remind me of unruly ponytails. From time to time, they toss these feathery appendages like irritable professors. In the early evening at the marsh edges the birds stoop over the water surface and examine it closely, as if on the lookout for a mistake in a student essay.

Occasionally, one acts decisively, plunging its beak down into the brown-green water. A moment later it is raised, dripping, and, four times out of five, the beak holds a frog, spread-eagled and firmly clamped. The luckless frog is given a quick and efficient pancake-like flip to adjust its position for swallowing before disappearing down the bird's throat. And then the hunt resumes.

I never tire of watching this, counting the spoonbills' hunting tallies. There is no shortage of frog snacks. One bird disposes of thirty two before deciding that it has eaten its fill. Occasionally the spoonbills are elsewhere, but the place is always occupied, sometimes by a shy glossy ibis, which stalks the rich hunting ground, dark and solitary.

Despite our hopes, the sun is too strong, so we can only venture out in the early morning and at the end of the day, spending the in-between time in the cool interior of the domátio, our rented room above a Greek family home. The mother brings us homemade cakes, warm and crumbly, and a daily jug of freshly pressed nectarine juice. We are charmed by her acts of kindness. Each day we parrot our gratitude in our limited Greek, 'Efharisto poli (Thank you very much).'

And so, the time passes, and we stay longer and longer, sedated by Greek ambrosial offerings. The still air of the afternoons stupefies us, and we pass them in a siesta-like state. For five days we linger in this land of lotus eaters, enjoying a paradise of food, birds and afternoon naps.

When we do make our evening tours of the lake, we look out for the late shift of pelicans that patrols the middle of the lake in an orderly line. Safely out of reach, the birds are unfazed by us as they glide over the smooth surface. Two kinds breed on the reservoir, on specially constructed rafts anchored at the centre of the lake. On the rafts the pelicans are less serene than on the water. Through our binoculars, we watch them fretting and squabbling over their nest sites.

One evening we drive out past the moored fishing boats, with their peeling paint. Lying inert, their only crew is a hush of roosting herons, egrets and pygmy cormorants, perched immobile on board. We stop the car at the far side of the reservoir, where we've noticed that the rows of brightly coloured bee-eaters like to congregate, lining up on the telegraph wires overhead. It's become a regular stopping place for us, so that we can watch them launch themselves in aerobatic pursuit of dragonflies and other flying insects.

This evening I am deeply engrossed in these aerial displays when, not far from the lake edge, the agitated behaviour of a grey heron catches my eye. The bird is hopping about in some tall grass with its wings partially open. There is a flurry of kicking legs and jabbing beak. I get a glimpse of the cause: a long, thick-bodied snake with a malevolent triangular head, possibly, a venomous horn-nosed viper.

After several moments of frantic engagement with its adversary, the heron seems to have gained the upper hand and takes off, struggling with the weighty, and still writhing, snake in its bill. It flies to a small island offshore and lands heavily. There the heron stands with the snake's large head pinned in its bill, while its body performs spirals in the air beneath. It appears confident, but the fight is not yet over. The snake rallies its forces and contorts wildly, like a lethal Medusan hair curl. It whips this way and that until it finds purchase by wrapping its muscular body around the length of the bird's bill, encasing it firmly in a tight coil.

This unexpected tactic startles the heron, and it is uncertain what to do. It is unable to stab, make a sound or shake the snake off. It seems to literally be a deadlock situation since, even if the snake is not dead, the heron's beak is certainly locked. But acting with impressive cunning, the bird immerses its packaged bill into the fast-flowing water at the edge of the island. To the snake, this must come as an ice-cold shock.

Raising its beak, the heron repeats its dunking strategy again and again. I watch, taut with suspense, and time stands still. After many immersions the snake is defeated and half-drowned. Its coils slacken and finally it gives up the fight and hangs limply from the heron's bill. Only then does the bird loosen its own pincer-like grip on the snake's head and start the difficult operation of swallowing its prey, a few centimetres at a time.

With the snake in its belly, the heron stands tall and victorious on its island for a few moments before flying off slowly towards the sinking sun. Life and death fights must be daily events in this richly populated corner of the animal kingdom.

I slowly let out my breath. Then I check my watch—the drama has taken twenty tense minutes. Inspired by what I have seen, my thoughts return to those meddling Greek deities. An imaginative explanation presents itself. Was it a resourceful heron? Or really a shape-shifting god in avian form? Whatever the truth, I am glad that I happened to be in the right place at the right time to witness the extraordinary event.

See Greece, Crete, Turkey, Egypt and Israel map on page 243.

The Misadventure of a Goose

candle flickers. An eye, a chin, a cheekbone: parts of faces become illuminated briefly. They belong to a group of pilgrims seated in a huddle around a low table; in front of them a circle of beers from which they take occasional sips. They are exchanging stories, straining to understand dialects and accents, which seem strange and incomprehensible to each other.

No, it is not medieval times but 2017. These modern-day pilgrims are gathered in a pub in the small village of Walsingham, a place lost in the heart of Norfolk. They are 'Weegies', they inform me. In other words, Glaswegians. They are resilient people with a unique sense of humour and a love of bantering, I discover. Travelling down from the far north of the country, they have driven in turn without stopping. I have travelled up from the other end of the country, an island off the south coast, taking a less demanding, if more complicated, option—a route involving a boat, a train, the Tube, a train again and then several local buses—to reach this place in the wilds of East Anglia. Like them, I have made a pilgrimage here.

I have come on an impulsive decision made in November. It is a solo venture and neither an obvious time of year nor a typical destination for today's pilgrim. Every year people flock in their hundreds of thousands to the pilgrimage hotspots of Rome and Jerusalem, and in springtime many more walk the now re-popularised El Camino routes which criss-cross the whole of Europe to converge at Santiago de Compostela in Spain. An antipathy for crowds, heavy backpacks and blisters has made me set my sights somewhat lower, on a location half-buried here in the fen country in the now barren brown fields of north Norfolk.

A few days ago I conducted a quick Google search, then with a strong magnifying glass found this tiny spot on the map. I realised that mid-November was the perfect time to come. The weather could be relied upon to be unreliable and I would avoid any possible encounters with a crowd. I rejected the idea of walking there, to avoid blisters. Robert Louis Stevenson went sojourning across France on a donkey and Che Guevara rode a motorbike across Latin America. Even if I wasn't following the perambulating example of the Canterbury pilgrims or John Bunyan's protagonist, my challenge would be tackling the cross-country transport system in the UK instead.

So I fill a small backpack—a suitcase doesn't seem to fit the image—and go online to buy a train ticket as far as Norwich. Then I check the timetables and set off on the start of my own Pilgrim's Progress.

In Norwich I discover that there is no direct bus service to Walsingham and, confusingly, there are two Walsinghams—Little Walsingham and Great Walsingham. 'Which one do you want?' the first of several bus drivers inquires of me in his smooth dipthong-less Norfolk accent. I make a choice. It doesn't matter, as fortunately they are not far apart—I will walk between them if necessary.

Several bus changes and many scenic village stops later, and with darkness falling, the last bus sets me down at a small triangular intersection, the centre of Little Walsingham, and I wander down the only street, a short stretch of timber-framed buildings, to look for my accommodation. I find the Pilgrim Hostel, register and, leaving my backpack in the reception office, cross a small courtyard to join the dinner queue in the refectory. There is hardly need of a queue, but I join the end, behind four talkative Glaswegians. It turns out that they are old hands at doing pilgrimages. This is the second day of their third trip to the shrines of Walsingham. I am very impressed.

Discovering that I am a total novice in the art of pilgrimage, they take me under their wing and over dinner instruct me as we slowly break through the language barrier. I learn about a Saxon chapel and a Holy House; the ruins of an Augustinian Priory, an ancient Marian shrine created from the vision of a noblewoman, visited and venerated for several hundred years in medieval England and as famous then as Rome and Jerusalem. Believers made long and arduous journeys on foot from all over England and farther afield to reach it. I am filled with awe as it dawns on me how many feet have trodden this way before mine. The search for spiritual meaning, purification and a fresh start drove tens of thousands of people to Walsingham down the ages, before eventually its statue and buildings were torn down and burnt during the Reformation. For the next few centuries the village and the ruins of its historic past slept undisturbed until, once again, the faithful began to visit it in the twentieth century. But I am still imagining those medieval pilgrims trudging a thousand footpaths across the landscape to pour into this small village from all directions. Inspired by my dinner companions, I begin planning. Tomorrow I will don my walking boots and head out across the dank and windy fields to follow the old Pilgrim's Way and visit the outlying shrines. And, like those before me, I will take home a souvenir pilgrim's badge as my tangible proof of visit.

We continue talking as we eat and are just starting the pudding course when it happens. Abruptly, we are plunged into darkness. Pilgrimages, ancient and modern, must meet such hazards, so we sit and wait, unfazed. Technology rescues us. Mobile phones are pulled out of pockets to shed light on our apple crumble and custard. Someone goes off to look for a fusebox. Coffee follows and our conversation flows out into the darkness. A box of handy devotional candles appears and soon a myriad of small lights adorn the refectory. Then a news update passes from table to table. It seems that fiddling with the fusebox has not solved the problem and someone has noticed that the lights are out in the entire village and even in the surrounding ones too. It's quite possible that normal service will not be resumed tonight. Taking up our candles, we tentatively step outside to experience this new world steeped in darkness. There is little to see at ground level, but, above, in the spangled autumn sky, the solicitous stars gaze down on us from their distant thrones. We feel small and insignificant, perhaps as did earlier visitors to the shrine. A reverential silence engulfs us as the universe awes us with its magnificent presence.

Humbled and slightly uncertain, we stand close together wondering what to do next. Someone makes a Glaswegian joke to break the eerie black silence. I don't get it, but then I didn't catch all the words. Someone else hits on the pilgrim's answer to all dilemmas sent to test, and we follow him in a stumbling, candlelit procession down to the pub at the street's intersection. Many of the villagers are there already. Candles are on every table and the hand-pumped beer is flowing. Gladdened by the company, we while away the next few hours, grappling with the task of human communication through our different vernaculars. Then with last orders called, we again form a ragged line and, with dripping candles, return to the hostel to finger-feel our way along the corridor walls to our rooms.

I wake in the morning and tentatively flick a switch. The lights come on as if nothing has happened. Power has been restored during the night. And what caused it? The engineers report that a migrating goose flew into an overhead power line, taking out the supply to a cluster of Norfolk villages and cooking itself to a crisp in the process. The Glaswegians and I part company after breakfast; they, to start the long drive back to Scotland, and I, to find the Pilgrim's Way. They ask me if I think I will return one day and I reply a little ruefully, 'Well, perhaps. It's too early to tell.' But I am already wondering what can possibly surpass the memory of last night. The candlelit procession to share a beer with new companions from a faraway place, all brought about by the misadventure of an errant goose.

See England map on page 241.

Lovestruck in Leningrad

Aside glance at the uniform and its occupant, the young Russian officer sitting next to me at the Moscow State Circus, was all it took. It was love at first sight. A totally unplanned event in my tourist itinerary.

It was the mid-1980s, time of Perestroika and Glasnost, wonderfully evocative words which had entered the English language overnight even if we weren't entirely sure what they meant. Gorbachev was in charge, and I was in Leningrad, as St Petersburg was then called, on a city visit meticulously managed by Intourist, the Soviet tour operator. I travelled there across the Baltic Sea by boat from Stockholm—an overnight crossing to Helsinki with a coachload of Swedes. Onboard we dined on smörgåsbord, a fitting choice, and had enjoyed a romantic sailing through the small pine-capped islands of the Swedish and Finnish archipelagos at dusk and dawn respectively. It was a propitious start.

In Helsinki, we transferred to a coach and drove towards the Finnish-Russian border. The landscape began to change as soon as we left the bright lights of central Helsinki. Block after block of grey monotone apartments caused me to nod off and for the next hour or so my head lolled uncomfortably against the pleated curtain of the coach window. When I woke we had reached the border and were being ordered off, so that our visas could be scrutinised and the coach thoroughly searched for the contraband that we were undoubtedly smuggling into Russia to sell on the black market. It hadn't occurred to me to bring cigarettes or spirits to subsidise my trip, and I was rather disappointed when the Russian border guards' search failed to reveal anything concealed by my fellow passengers either. We should then have been waved on our way, but Soviet protocol demanded otherwise. The coach was cranked up on a vehicle lift so that its underside could be checked—presumably for more contraband, rather than to inspect its roadworthiness. Some time later we were grudgingly allowed back on the federal highway to Leningrad, a mere 250 miles away—just a Lilliputian footstep into the sprawling expanse of Russia. There were no further stops.

Over the next two days we 'got to know' Leningrad, enjoying the officially sanctioned experience that we were given by our Soviet hosts. Every morning after breakfast the red and white tour bus and its glum driver were waiting outside the hotel. Our guide, unsmiling in her ill-fitting grey Intourist uniform, would bid us 'Good morning' and then wrestle with the crack-ling on-board microphone as we settled into our seats for that day's magical mystery tour. We referred to it as a mystery tour, because no advance programme was available, although it did become possible to predict some regular features of the daily tour. Usually included was some instruction in the government buildings of Leningrad and their bureaucratic functions. I tried hard to concentrate but am not sure how many of the salient details I retained.

The tours of the squares were a bit easier as each was crowned with the statue of an important historical figure. I successfully identified the first one as Lenin. The next one may have been Lenin too. It was a bit confusing as several appeared to have been cast from the same mould from the neck downwards. All adopted a similar dramatic stance—in mid stride and scowling into the distance. Their coats were invariably flung open. I decided that this must be an allusion to the formidable winds of the Russian steppes—and an arm, usually the right one, was outstretched. At the end of the arm there was often an accusative finger, which seemed to be pointing at me. A sense of guilt crept over me with each new statue we saw. I was relieved when the guide informed us that they were pointing out the future path to economic prosperity.

Government buildings and Soviet squares aside, the tours did contain some anticipated sights. There was a memorable visit to the Hermitage Museum and its huge collection of art and cultural artefacts, and an evening drive along the Nevsky Prospekt, the city's most famous street, lit up along its entire length. There was also an unexpected stop at an orthodox church. Good, I thought, we're going to see some icons. I entered, expecting a candlelit interior heavy with incense and walls adorned with devotional paintings of saints whose penetrating eyes meet yours wherever you are standing. At last we would see something from the pre-communist era, a taste of the old Russia and maybe even a glimpse into the Slavic soul. But sadly, there were no icons and not a whiff of incense. The building was no longer functioning as a church and was instead housing the Museum of the History of Religion and its dusty display cases.

Things began to look up on the last night of our tour. The guide proudly informed us that as a special treat we had a choice for our final evening's entertainment. We could choose to see a performance of the Bolshoi Ballet—which came highly recommended by our guide—or see the Moscow State Circus. Unaccustomed to treats or a choice, many of our group vacillated wildly between the possibilities but were eventually persuaded to choose the Bolshoi. Three of us decided on the circus. Our tour guide was displeased as this meant organising two separate sets of tickets as well as minders to escort us. Being both non-compliant and in the minority, the circus goers took second place in the arrangements and so we arrived at the venue late.

Everyone was already seated and the show had just begun. In the very full auditorium there were no free places together so we were separated and quickly distributed to three empty seats. The minder ushered me to one in the middle of a back row. No one was happy about the disturbance. 'Izvinitje, izvinitje,' I excused myself as I squeezed along the narrow line, ejecting several Russian families from their seats in the process, and trampling on the food and drink they had carefully arranged on the floor in front of them. I reached my place, sat down and it was then that I turned to flash an apologetic smile at my handsome neighbour. He was looking straight ahead.

The circus did not disappoint. Act after act bewitched us. A troupe of clowns poured out into the ring and began to juggle, then pushed and pulled each other around in slapstick fashion to loud encouragement from the younger members of the audience. Then followed a band of Cossacks in their wide trousers and flapping tunics. They stood astride their galloping horses and whirled themselves dangerously over the saddles or hung by a hand from the flanks of their mounts as they dashed around in circles. There was a collective holding of breath as trapeze artists performed gravity-defying acrobatics with split-second timing and caught each other in mid-air.

Something also caught my attention in the aisle. It was a large round spotlight anchored to the floor and focused on the stage. Behind it sat a babushka, a rotund Russian grandmother complete with headscarf. She was the spotlight operator. Every so often she laid down her knitting and flicked a switch or changed the angle of the spotlight.

But recalling it decades later, one memory eclipsed all of this: the handsome young Russian officer sitting at my side. Immaculate in every respect in his pine green uniform, I surreptitiously admired each detail: from the embossed brass buttons on his jacket to the impressive high-peaked cap with black visor, carefully positioned on his lap. On the green band that encircled its brim there was an emblematic red star set on a gold badge. Unable to resist, I took a quick peek at his profile and noted the carefully combed fair hair curling against his forehead and his clear blue eyes, shining with enjoyment. In that instance, I was smitten. Perhaps I had been intoxicated by the excitement of the circus or just captivated by a man in uniform. It didn't matter. Here beside me was the face of the real Russia I'd been looking for. But I could only idolise from afar. We neither spoke, nor exchanged a meaningful look. So dear reader, I regret to say that I did not marry him. In fact, I never saw him again. Unlike me, he only had eyes for the circus.

See Sweden, Norway, Finland and Russia map on page 248.

The Mystery of a Nudge
in the Night

Every three or four years there is a population explosion. In 1994 there was one, and I know this because I was there.

On summer nights, where the Arctic Circle severs the neck of Norway like a guillotine, the world is bathed in a mysterious twilight. Sleep does not come naturally here. Around midnight, in a forest next to a surging river, I tossed and turned, blaming my restlessness on the tent—erected hastily, the ground lumpy and my sleeping bag constricting me like an anaconda. The world outside was awake and disturbed too. I gave up wrestling with the sleep angel and lay, listening to its sounds. My back felt uncomfortable and suddenly twitched. Once and then twice I felt a small shove, a clearly discernible nudge from below, too gentle and subtle for an earth tremor—but what then? A mole or a mouse burrowing beneath me perhaps? The nudging stopped. I turned on my side, pulled the sleeping bag up over my ears. The sleep angel won, and I finally drifted off to the sound of the muffled roar of the river.

The next morning the natural world was alive and bright at an unsociably early hour. The rich tang of damp forest humus filled the air. Scrambling out of the tent, I set off to collect a few bilberries to pep up my morning porridge. When I returned, my companions were up and boiling water for tea. Over breakfast we planned the day's walk through the forest. We packed up the tents and brushed out the previous day's accumulated bits of twig and leaf from our socks and boots. Then we were on our way.

The path we had chosen wound its way through a tangle of trees and over lumps and bumps created by ancient Caledonian rocks bulging out from the earth. Small thickets of robust bilberry lined the route, cheering us on with their red and green bunting-like leaves and irresistible berries. It wasn't long before our hands and mouths were stained purple.

After an hour or so we paused for a break and took out our water bottles. Birdsong was coming from a tree nearby. Rummaging in our packs, we found our binoculars and scanned the branches to locate its source. I was startled by an abrupt movement at my side. It was my companion's head, jerking downwards in surprise to look at the path. My gaze followed. A colourful furry bundle tumbled over his boot and disappeared into a bilberry thicket. We bent down and peered deep into the bush. At ground level, our faces were met by a high-pitched screech and then the small bundle mock-charged us. Its tiny black eyes glittered with rage and a set of equally small yellow incisors bared up at us from an angry open mouth. This unexpected display of feistiness took us by surprise. I was still trying to decide what I was looking at when my companion exclaimed in delight, 'It's a lemming!'

Unimpressed by us or my friend's identification skills, our plucky foe backed into the security of the bilberries, still screeching and bearing its fangs at us. With two goliaths barring its way out, it realized it was in a tight corner and decided that making itself scarce was the better part of valour. The bush trembled a couple of times as a lemming in a hurry negotiated its interior, seeking an alternative exit. Then suddenly the bundle shot out and away into the forest. It was gone.

This was the first of many encounters we had with members of the *Lemmus lemmus* species that summer holiday. They ran, leapt, danced or sauntered across our path everywhere. Sometimes they froze in front of us, hoping to go unnoticed. For every lemming we saw, no doubt a further twenty were hiding nearby waiting to dash across the path. All were lemmings on a mission, driven by a need, an urge, a message communicated on the lemming bush telegraph—who knows how but they knew. Going where lemmings had gone before, they were following the example of lemming communities since, well, the dawn of lemming communities. *Lemmus lemmus*, or the Norwegian lemming, is a hamster-like rodent related to voles. I discovered that it has many exotic cousins with intriguing names such as the bog lemming, the wood lemming, the steppe lemming, and the Arctic lemming, which turns white in winter. *Lemmus lemmus*, is, however, the 'true' lemming, the one known for its periodic mass migrations or so-called suicide runs.

From our many meetings that summer, I got to know the creature well, both temperamentally and physically. Although smaller in size, its coloration reminded me of a scruffy pet guinea-pig I once owned: black, ginger and white. It wears these three colours in a rather untidy tufty coat that appears to have seen better days. Beneath the overcoat are four stubby but surprisingly agile little legs, and a short tail. Explosions of its population occur every few years when its numbers increase to a point where there is insufficient food for all. And so their only option is to migrate en masse in search of new territory. They travel by day, but also by night. Now I understood that mysterious nudge in the night; it was a lemming on the move, passing beneath my tent and attempting to shove me out of the way. This was going to be a useful conversation starter for a dinner party one day. I also found out that lemmings not only migrate over land but they can also swim across lakes and rivers. Oceans pose a bigger problem, so lemmings that leap off cliff edges are not suicidal but have just taken a wrong turn somewhere along the way.

That explosive summer of 1994 I fraternized a lot with the lemming population and felt rather privileged to have witnessed this remarkable event for myself!

See Sweden, Norway, Finland and Russia map on page 248.

Marking Time

31

A muted peal of the first church bells carries across the rooftops and filters through the closed shutters of my apartment in Via Vicenza. I turn on my mattress towards the window. Soon there will be others ringing out from across the city to announce the hour of the Mass. It's impossible to sleep any longer, and I've no wish to. A sunbeam is bouncing on the stone floor, one that has found its way in through a broken slat. Sunday morning in Urbs Aeterna, the eternal city, as the ancients called Rome. Today is a special day and I'm going to make a favourite journey. And since it's another hot day, I'd better get out early.

I'm alone in the apartment. My Italian flatmate, Francesco, has gone home to Calabria for a long weekend. 'Buon fine settimana (Have a good weekend),' he said, opening the front door to leave. Then his brown eyes twinkled, 'y non dimenticare la spazzatura, Julie.' It's a weekly chore that neither of us seems capable of remembering. This morning I mustn't forget to take the rubbish down to the communal bin. Soon I am ready, but first I set the moka pot on the stove for the first caffeine hit of the day.

A few moments later and a prolonged throaty gurgle tells me that the water has percolated through to the coffee grounds. I breathe in the familiar rich aroma filling the kitchen and pour a stream of hot brown liquid into a small cup. Then the ritual. In a spoon, carefully lowered onto the surface, I slowly dissolve two lumps of sugar. Two miniature icebergs that calve into a dark espresso sea. That should be sweet enough. A quick stir, four gulps and the coffee is gone.

Outside, the city has stirred, woken by the church bells, like me. In Piazza Indipendenza I arrive just in time to see the number 75 coughing out a spume of exhaust as it leaves the bus stand. My arm is raised to the driver, but he ignores me. The bus doors are closed.

'Cazzarola! (Drat!).' You would think that today, of all days… A backup plan then. Into the maze of back streets behind Stazione Roma Termini. A right, another right, and then a left—my feet know the way so well they carry me there without instructions, to the central railway station, with Piazza Cinquecento sprawling out in front of it.

The bus terminal is in the middle of the piazza, where a herd of immobile ATAC buses are gathered like sleeping orange caterpillars. Two are slowly crawling away. One lurches out into the circling traffic; the other is wobbling around a distant corner and out of sight. Thankfully, neither is the 64. Otherwise, I might have had a long wait for the next one. I find the right bay and wait beside a green pole.

A spiral of dry dust particles is pirouetting beautifully in the morning sunshine in front of me, a celebratory dance as I start my journey. A man passes holding *Il Messaggero*. I forgot to buy mine, at the newspaper stand I passed on the way. Well, I wouldn't have much time to read it anyway. And too late. I remember about the spazzatura. Never mind—there's always tomorrow. Just then a 64 pulls in and releases a long drawn-out hiss as its doors jerk open.

No one gets off except the driver. Nearly all of them take a customary cigarette break at Termini. He's left the doors open, so I step inside. It's empty except for a handful of tourists studying their maps. A day of sightseeing lies ahead of them. I expect they're on their way to San Pietro and the Vatican Museums—the end of the line for the 64.

Something is happening on the bus in the next bay. Inside a throng of animated elderly Italian ladies are moving about and chattering loudly, dressed in black widows' weeds and laden with bags, purses and armfuls of chrysanthemums, fresh from the florists. I watch them twist in their seats to greet each other and exchange their gossip. They'll be going to the cemetery for the weekly tidying of graves. Bereavement bands them together. And flowers. I smile. I will have my own later, although not chrysanthemums.

Some Italians do not seem to be genetically wired with volume control. Our driver is gesticulating and in loud conversation with a fellow ATAC driver. I catch snippets of the exchange: 'ma che cretino! (what an idiot!)' and 'che cazzo vuole lui? (what the hell does he want?).' I wonder who they're taking about. But mostly, I enjoy the semaphoric show, until my driver throws down his cigarette butt and boards the bus again.

A long flouncing colourful skirt catches my eye as we pull away. Like me, it's owner is not a native here. The Italians call them zingari (gypsies), so-called Romani, but not from Rome at all—migrants belonging to an ethnic group said to have come from India originally. Now in the 1980s they can be found all across southern Europe, living on the streets by day. I don't know where they go at night. The woman has a long heavy plait of black hair and is wandering haphazardly through the square with a cupped hand, begging as she goes. Termini is her patch. I've seen her here before, pressing sprigs of heather onto people and asking for money.

But it's some of their children you have to watch out for—often dishevelled with deft fingers. They home in on the newly arrived tourists. I saw them surround a lost-looking backpacker once, hold ragged pieces of cardboard up to distract him while one of them filched his wallet. Then they were gone. He didn't even realise what had happened until they were halfway across the piazza. He ran after them shouting, but it was too late.

We've reached Piazza della Repubblica and the bus is circling the ever-gushing Fountain of the Naiads in a merry-go-round of celebration. As usual, the four water nymphs are enveloped in a cloud of water mist. I grab the seat in front and smile as another lurch sends us swinging into Via Nazionale. The bus comes to a stop in front of Banco di Roma—closed today, of course—and we take on more passengers. Another parting hiss and we are sucked into the growing lake of Sunday morning traffic. Honking cars and whining scooters, all being channelled down this long road. Where is it all going to on a Sunday morning? Anyway, I'm in no hurry. We crawl along mid-stream until we reach the end of Nazionale and start a winding descent. I'll need to change bus before too long. I could intercept a 70 or the 170, perhaps? But, I'll stay on the 64 for a bit longer, at least until it gets too crowded with tourists.

Two squares come in a rush. The first is Largo Argentina—the archaeological ruins at its centre are where Caesar was murdered, they say. But now it's a sanctuary—for cats. The maimed, the blind, the homeless. The word spreads fast on the cat grapevine and they all come here. As we rumble past, I spy one of the gattare in attendance—a cat lady, leaning over the balustrade with a bag of food in her hand. Then we are in Piazza Venezia. It's huge and dominated by the Wedding Cake. La Torta Nuziale, as the Italians call it, or sometimes the typewriter, L'Olivetti, because of its overindulgence in tiered columns. Actually, this imposing white monument is dedicated to Vittorio Emanuele II, Italy's first king after unification.

We stop for more tourists to climb aboard, and I make a decision and get off. I can't see a 70 or any other bus heading in my direction, so I walk to the far end of the square, towards the wide stone steps that fan out lazily as they mount to the Piazza Campidoglio, one of the many Michelangelo masterpieces scattered across the capital. Up in the piazza, the Capitoline Museums will have already opened their doors to the first visitors. I too have wandered down the lines of marble busts of Roman statesmen inside and been struck by how their ancient faces bear the same worldly-wise expressions as those of their modern descendants outside in the streets today.

I'm thinking of hopping onto another bus on the Via Del Teatro di Marcello. But which one? Will a 280 take me in the right direction? I'm unsure. Abruptly, I change my mind again. There's too much traffic now. I'll find a quieter route, on foot. I cross the road and enter the web of narrow lanes that forms the Angelo, the old Jewish quarter, full of small greengrocers, trattoria and cafes. I pass through the lingering aroma of sweet vegetables and freshly baked pastries to the Tevere, Rome's meandering river Tiber, across which my destination lies. But on the way, I can't resist stopping at a bar in the Angelo for another dose of caffeine and a couple of cornetti—a late breakfast.

A last twisting street brings me out of the maze alongside the river and right beside the Isola Tiberina. It's a boat-shaped island spanning the Tiber with a bridge on either side connecting to each bank. I read that there was once an ancient temple here to Asclepius, the Greek God of Medicine, and somewhere there's a stone with a snake symbol carved into it. I've searched twice but not found it yet. As I walk past, I look across at the small hospital lying at the island's centre, remembering, with a smile, the name of its religious founders: the Fatebenefratelli—the do-good brothers.

I've reached Ponte Garibaldi now. Not far to go. The final part of my journey takes me across the bridge, over the swirling brown waters of the Tiber, and into Trastevere—one of the oldest parts of Rome. Nearby is one of my favourite restaurants. I'll go there later for lunch. They do a very good Pasta alla Gricia, or, maybe, because it's a special day, I'll have Tagliatelle al Salmone. But I mustn't overindulge—I'm eating out with friends again this evening.

The imposing church of San Crisogono comes into view in Piazza Sonnino. Before I moved into central Rome, I used to escape there at the end of my teaching day, breaking the long bus ride back to my shared digs in the suburbs. I still visit; the church offers a welcome sanctuary from the noise, summer heat and chaos of life outside. Half an hour enclosed in the coolness of its silent stone interior restores some order to my world. But it's not my destination today.

Instead, I turn right and cut across the square of Santa Maria in Trastevere to Via della Scala. A gentle uphill walk and I arrive at number 24 Largo Cristina di Svezia. The wrought iron gates of the Orto Botanico, Rome's Botanical Gardens, stand open in front of me. I step inside. Thirty-one. I can hardly believe it! To misquote Dylan Thomas, 'It's my thirty-first year to heaven' and I've come here to mark my birthday. I will spend it in the Orto Botanico, one of the most special places in all of Rome.

See Italy map on page 240.

The Last Wood Turner

C aptured in a shaft of sunlight in the doorway, a spiral of fine dust was slowly dancing, recreating the harmony of the spheres. Outside in the narrow, cobbled street, I stopped to admire it in childlike wonder. A whiff of sweet resin tickled my nostrils—newly sawn pine wood—and the scent drew me closer. I was feeling hot and weary, having lost my way in the winding backstreets of Toledo. The open doorway was inviting.

The interior was dark and my eyes took time to adjust. An elaborate small cage, entirely constructed of wood, stood on a table just inside the entrance. On parallel perches, facing each other, sat two goldfinches. They had seen better days. Scrawny, but with bright eyes alert in their scarlet masks, they observed me observing them.

'Son mis amigos: Chico y Chica (They are my friends: Boy and Girl),' a disembodied voice informed me, adding that they were eleven years old. Eleven years old? Incredulous that such a tiny bird could live so long, I turned towards the source of the voice. It belonged to Luis, Tornero y Artesano de la Madera, a traditional wood turner and artisan, whose workshop I had entered.

He stepped out of the darkness in a work apron, his shirt sleeves rolled to the elbow, the hairs on his forearms coated in amber-coloured wood dust. Surrounding us was a cornucopia of woodcraft—chairs, hat-racks, candlesticks, table legs, spinning tops, doorstops, even a church monstrance. Luis had made them all with his woodturning machine.

'Ha hecho muchas cosas (You've made a lot),' I said, looking around slightly disoriented as I tried to take stock of everything.

It was a family business, passed down through grandfather and father—abuelo y padre—and finally to Luis himself, now nearly fifty years in the trade, he said proudly.

'Y sus hijos? (And your sons)' I enquired. No, there was no one else to take it on, he explained. In two years' time everything would be gone. He gestured emphatically sweeping his work-worn hands in front of him, splaying their cracked fingers. The work is hard and bad for the eyes. He paused before continuing and I noticed one of his pale grey eyes squinting slightly leftwards. Sometimes the concentration leaves you feeling crazy at the end of the day. Now there was only him left but he was proud to be the last of his profession still working in Toledo.

Then, in a matter of fact voice: I don't make much money. The tourists want things cheaper or just take photos. They don't understand how many hours it takes to make something. I stroked the curved neck of a wooden heron and nodded, staying silent. Only he was left now—the words hung in the air between us.

Then a shadow severed the sunlight in the doorway, dispelling the moment. Two more visitors entered the workshop. Some potential customers, perhaps. I smiled at Luis, thanking him. 'Buen trabajo,' my parting wish. Grasping my hand firmly he shook it and in a clear voice said, 'Adios.' As I went out into the heat of the cobbled street once more, one of the goldfinches was preening its dusty feathers.

See Spain and Canary Islands map on page 238.

On Crocodile Beach

One last curving sweep and the passenger plane crosses over the thin white line where tropical beach meets sapphire-blue sea. Then the island of Borneo falls away out of sight. I am flying home on Royal Brunei Airlines, having come to the end of my teaching contract in this small oil-rich country, the size of Devon.

Much of my time there was spent perspiring in a humid classroom, as I attempted to teach English to 36 Malay-speaking school children. But as the plane steadily climbs into the blue beyond, the view from the porthole triggers a slideshow of memories, flickering out from a cranky old Kodak projector that has suddenly jerked into action. One by one, a chain of flashbacks passes through my mind, taking me back; not to the classroom, but to the beach.

First slide: Pantai Meraggang, or as everyone calls it, Crocodile Beach. I am de-stressing after a day in the classroom, basking a few metres offshore in the warm evening waters. A ripple on the surface spreads out like a ribcage in the water, moving in my direction—a sea snake! It zigzags along, trailing its distinctive flat tail in the wake. Highly poisonous, even if it's small mouth would struggle to bite me. I get out of the water faster than you can say 'Bandar Seri Begawan'—the name of the capital of Brunei, where I have been living, although no one uses its full name; it's simply BSB.

A click and the magazine changes slide. Crocodile Beach again. A different evening. Two young Malaysian women are standing waist-deep in the sea, modestly wrapped in wet sarongs. They observe me as I swim a few lazy strokes then turn to float on my back. I notice them watching and smile back.

Encouraged, they ask, 'Please show us swimming.' I oblige, demonstrating first the arm and then the leg actions for breast-stroke and soon they are laughing and spluttering as they try to copy my movements. Crocodile Beach is a place where the unexpected can happen, even an impromptu swimming lesson.

A new slide. I am walking beside the sea, stopping occasionally to turn over some flotsam with my foot. I have never much liked just lying on the beach. Swimming and walking are better. The rhythmic sound that accompanies me as I walk is like a meditation mantra, repeated and repeated, the rattle of shingle being dragged back and forth on the seashore.

I pause and my foot combs the surface of the sand, revealing something. A message in a bottle, perhaps? No. It is a small shell, half a bivalve and a delicate shade of pink. I see there are more and start collecting them. Soon I have a handful of pink gleaming baby teeth, enough to serve the dental needs of a gapping crocodile.

Click, ker-chunk, and another slide is delivered. I have walked around a small headland on the beach and into some mangroves where the tide is out, exposing a maze of protruding stumps and knobbly periscopes—a jungle of tidal forest trees and their aerial roots. Glassy-eyed grey mudskippers are hopping out of my way, and the spongy mud of the marbled sand-cake I cross is sucking at my feet. My hands are full again. This time with fragments of ancient pottery of different kinds. Blue and white, iron-painted and pale green glazed shards.

Remnants of the lost cargoes of maritime traders, they have been washed ashore from the wrecks that lie in an ocean grave-yard, somewhere offshore at the bottom of the South China sea. I retrace my steps, with a pocketful of casualties of tropical storm, pirate attack or hidden reef. In the plane's overhead compartment, my cabin bag holds a small selection of my best finds—some travel mementos are coming home with me.

Next slide please. More rich pickings from Crocodile Beach. Last night there was another tropical cyclone, and now the sea-shore is strewn with new arrivals. I'm looking at a mat of dead and living plant material. Some are opportunist waterborne travellers; giant seeds dispersed from their deltas out into the open sea; they have floated far in search of a place to put down roots. Here is the tufted fruit of a Nipa palm, one of the oldest plants in the world. It began its life inland beside a river in an enormous sibling cluster of fist-sized, fluted carpels.

And there is a pong-pong fruit, as it is called in Malay. A woody ball of a seed case, the size of a grape. Its surface is covered in an intricate network of wavy ridges, and if I could break its tough exterior, there is a mass of seeds inside. Curiously, if I can find a pong-pong tree between 9.30–10.00 a.m. I could witness its flowers opening, or so I've read.

The storm has also thrown up a Dungun seed. Smooth to the touch and a rich mocha brown, it has a very distinctive keel on one side and has ridden the waves like a boat, bobbing around in the water for weeks or even months on end before reaching this shore.

Another click. But the show is over. This time, it's one of the cabin crew starting up the onboard intercom, 'Good Evening, ladies and gentlemen. In a few minutes, the flight attendants will be passing around the cabin to offer you hot or cold drinks and a light meal. Meanwhile, please relax and enjoy the flight.'

I reset my seat to the upright position and turn to look out of the porthole at the blue horizon. I never did see a crocodile on the beach bearing its name, nor did I find a message in a bottle, but I am not disappointed. The beach gave me other treasures to take home.

See Borneo and East Malaysia map on page 242.

Oracle

The man in the doorway with the twirled black moustache beckons me. My eyes want to look away but are
held fast. Two waxed ends dip slightly over his top lip.
It is fastidiously groomed: a Turkish love affair. I'm standing
outside a small carpet shop in Didim on the Aegean coast, and
the owner of the shop, and of the moustache, is appraising me
as a potential customer for one of his hand-woven rugs.

From Istanbul to Didim, a network of air-conditioned coaches
has transported me across the heart of Turkey. In the last bus I
sat behind the driver, feeling queasy as it lurched from side to
side around each curve of the winding road. Like every other
driver here, this one had a small blue amulet swinging erratically
in front of his windscreen. The Turkish evil eye. A charm to
guard against evil spirits intent on causing harm. Superstitious
nonsense? More than once I found myself hoping its protection
covered road accidents.

The final straight stretch of the route came as a welcome gas-
tric relief. I watched through the dusty window as kilometre after
kilometre of shimmering hot sand and azure-blue Mediterranean
Sea passed by, while on the roadside, archaeological debris lined
the route; tumbledown columns and pedestals lay abandoned. I

caught only glimpses of their former beauty in flashes of white alabaster gleaming through the rampant vegetation that clawed and clambered over them.

Following the coastal route, I have joined the tide of humanity that has flowed this way over the millennia. There are signs of their past presence everywhere, of the ancient Greeks who colonised and made their homes here, and of Crusaders, fired up with religious fervour and bound for Jerusalem. Then, more recently, twentieth century hedonists and sun seekers. Behind them, they all have left their signature in a column, a castle or a condom.

Sometimes I stop and linger for a while, to explore a place before moving on. This time, I am breaking my journey in ancient Didyma to visit the Sanctuary of Apollo. Long ago others came before me from Asia Minor to consult the resident oracle and find out what the future held in store. The temple priests and suppliants to the Greek god Apollo are long gone, but their presence could still be felt as I wandered through the rows of Ionian columns. And perhaps the oracle is still listening. Should I ask a question? Do I even want to know my future?

From his doorstep, Mehmet of the Moustache turns on some Turkish charm and with a gracious smile invites me into his shop, Best Didim Carpets and Export. 'Come please. You are welcome. Hoşgeldin.'

Shopkeepers here are all well-practised in the art of beguilement, and I have been enticed into many an Aladdin's cave of carpets during this trip. I make some feeble protestations: I have no money; I have no space in my pack for a souvenir rug; no thank you, I do not need one exported to my home country. But in the end, I accept the invitation to step inside, making it clear that I shall not buy.

I slip off my sandals and leave them at the entrance. Then I pause for a toe-stretching moment. My liberated feet enjoy the coolness of the springy carpet pile, while my eyes gradually adjust from the bright sun outside to the shady shop interior. A rug-scape surrounds me. Multi layered tumuli, mound upon mound of heaped rugs, in all directions. Along two of the walls stands a stockade of upright rolled carpets, enclosing the centre like a fortress. A faded picture of Atatürk, founding father of the Turkish Republic, looks down benignly over the carpet topography.

I cross the room and sit on a rug at Mehmet's invitation, taking care to arrange my legs neatly to the side and hide the soles of my feet, so as not to offend Turkish sensibilities. The conversation follows the usual format. First some polite questions from Mehmet: where am I from, where am I going, what are my impressions of Turkey? Then he deftly turns the conversation around to carpets. I become the student and my instruction begins. I am not entirely ignorant. It is a lesson I have received several times before.

First the most beautiful rugs are laid out for me to admire. Those of hand-spun wool or silk. These are authentic Anatolian rugs, Mehmet explains proudly, as we examine each one in turn.

'Çok güzel (Lovely),' I murmur, appreciatively.

His are made only by the women from the local villages and towns of the Konya region. I interrupt to tell him that I was in Konya just a few days ago, visiting the tomb of Mevlana, Sufi prophet and founder of the whirling dervishes. Mehmet nods, accepting the digression, then decides that this is a good moment to let his carpets work their magic on me. He leaves me in their charge and goes off to make some tea. Turkish hospitality requires it. The visitor must be treated as 'the guest sent by God'.

My thoughts stay in Konya, recalling the Muslim pilgrims I saw paying their respects at the tomb. They were on the Haj and on their way to Mecca, the men dressed in tan-coloured suits, the women in white. A wall inscription of the prophet's words was there, no doubt for the benefit of visiting westerners like me. It has remained in my mind: 'You come to me to feel your own experience. You are a lover of your own emotion.'

Yes, perhaps it's true. While staying in a small guesthouse, an old lady, grandmother of the owner, poured me a coffee prepared Turkish style: boiled and gritty. Afterwards, she read my future in the grounds at the bottom of the cup. She saw a flying bird and a ring which spoke of more travel and a marriage proposal. I could see only muddy coffee grounds. But I nodded and, seeing that she was in deadly earnest, I peered again into my cup, willing myself to believe it might be true.

Mehmet disturbs my reverie. He is carrying a small silver salver with two delicate tulip-shaped glasses. But the liquid in them is not the bronze colour of çay, Turkish tea. It is light amber, and there is the scent of something sweetly familiar that wafts from it. Mint. A refreshing change. I take a sip and again utter my stock Turkish phrase for many a situation: 'Çok güzel.'

We settle back into more carpet talk: the nitty-gritty of intricate knots and natural dyes. Some runners are brought out. I admire their colours: cobalt blue, verdant green and deep red. And here and there are special silver or gold threads woven into the design. The time passes. Our glasses are empty now, and I should be moving on. When I apologise again to Mehmet for not buying one of his beautiful carpets, repeating my usual excuses, he accepts it with a mask of Turkish politeness. I cannot see behind his mesmerising moustache to know whether he really minds that he has given me both time and tea in exchange for a no-sale.

But, at the doorway, as I slip my sandals back on, I hear his parting words, 'You will buy a carpet.' I am puzzled. Is it a question, an exhortation or is he foretelling the future? His intonation gives nothing away. I smile, sceptically. But the oracle never speaks falsely. Somewhere, in another town, another carpet shop, the charm of another Turkish salesman, a glass of çay and the beauty of a small honey-coloured prayer rug all combine to break my resolve and fulfil his prophecy. I buy one. It seems it was my destiny.

See Greece, Crete, Turkey, Egypt and Israel map on page 243.

Musical Postcards from India

Postcard 1: Ticket to ride

I'm boarding an Air India flight with my cabin bag crammed with farewell presents and mixed feelings. After two years in Japan, it's time to go home. Roughly halfway along an imaginary line in the sky stretching between Japan and the UK lies India. So, it's where I'm making my stopover.

Sayonara Japan. No more oriental rituals. I've made my last formal bow when being introduced and I've accepted my last heated hand flannel at the local sushi bar I frequented. With some regret, I'm leaving behind the delicate aroma of green tea and the subtle hay-like scent of the tatami mats in my flat. In India I will start to attune my ears to English again. And I am looking forward to a curry, and a cup of normal black tea with milk that tastes of home.

The flight is packed, and as I make my way through a tubular Aladdin's cave to aisle seat 55D, I don't feel as if I'm on an aeroplane at all. The cabin interior is vibrant with colourful decoration. Exotic figures, half-man half-beast, dance along the entire length of its walls, in pastel pink and lime green. Even the portholes are decorated with elaborate tracings of cusped or pointed arches.

I'm on a motorised magic carpet with wings, surrounded by stories from Hindu mythology and about to be whisked from Narita airport to New Delhi, my destination on the Indian subcontinent some 5000 kilometres away. I find 55D and settle in, moving the seat to the upright position ready for take-off as a stewardess in a red sari, her dark eyes outlined in kohl, leans towards me with a tray of tantalising Indian sweets wrapped in cellophane twists.

Postcard 2: While my guitar gently weeps

It's the season of monsoon rains—not the best time to be travelling overland down to Bombay, as my end destination is called in the early 1980s, now Mumbai. My route will be a caterpillar trail of journeys made by train, bus, three-wheeler rickshaw or whatever means presents itself. But my first stop is Delhi. After the shiny clockwork modernity of economically-booming Japan, India's capital is a worn-out piece of machinery, frantically trying to keep pace with the rest of the world. The chaos comes as a shock.

Stepping out from the hotel onto the street is like a Dantesque descent into the underworld, and my senses are assaulted in an instant—a hellish noise of honking horns and squealing brakes. A sharp contrast to Japan. The smell of diesel fumes is overwhelming. And as for the sights on the street, they provide a very alternative kind of tourist experience. Despite the rain, a clamour of street children have appeared, with outstretched hands, barefoot and dressed in torn and faded hand-me-downs. Some arrive with smaller siblings clamped to their sides.

'Helloo, Missus. How are you? Rupee plees,' they beg. I walk on, a few coins lighter, but every sheltered niche or doorway contains someone holding out a bowl or a hand—a mother with an unhealthy whining child or a disabled person on a cardboard mat, minus a leg or an arm. Opportunistic flies crawl all over the poverty and sickness that paves my way, and soon all my small change is gone.

I'm making slow progress. I want to escape the rain splash from passing traffic and avoid being swallowed up in the wave of suffering humanity on the pavement. So, on impulse I jump into the nearest vacant rickshaw. It proves to be the easiest way of exploring Delhi. From the segregated safety of a pedicab seat, I can sightsee the Red Fort, the Qutab Minar minaret and the majestic India Gate, watching a river of destitute humans wash by me, while periodically experiencing, like every other tourist here, twinges of guilt.

Postcard 3: With love from me to you

I t's day four and I'm glad to have left the mayhem of Delhi behind me. I've arrived in Agra, some 200 kilometres to the south, where I have stopped to see the Taj Mahal. I've booked my place on a tour tomorrow morning. After a restless night under a broken ceiling fan, I order tea from room service, and the boy comes bearing a tray with just a large teapot, a cup and saucer.

When he has left, I raise the teapot lid and am surprised to see that it is not filled with tea but a clay-brown liquid. I tentatively dip my small finger in, lick it and grimace. Sweet, with a faint flavour of tea, which, it seems, has been mixed with condensed milk. Oh well, I suppose I'd better get used to it or drink it black from now on. I pour out a cupful and gulp it down, trying not to let the cloying taste linger too long in my mouth.

In the afternoon I wander in a small, wooded park I found, by chance, near my hotel. It's quiet and there are no children besieging me. Or so I think, but then a small boy appears from behind a tree. He is not begging or hawking anything but stands in front of me with a shy smile. Perhaps he's a young entrepreneur with a new tactic? He holds out his hand. But it is not for money.

In his palm is a gift: a small round stone, the size of a walnut. Its exterior is almost translucent. Hesitantly, I take it from him, puzzled, and his smile grows. Then he says something in Hindi and takes it back. He squats down, puts the stone on the ground and takes a larger rock. I watch as he brings it down with force onto the smaller one, which neatly splits in two. He places the halves in my hand and raises his expectant eyes to meet my confused ones. I look down again. And then I understand.

Inside, both halves are hollow but lined with sparkling quartz crystals. It's a geological treasure—a nodule of rock, quite bland on the outside but concealing a hidden beauty of nature. How did he know what it contained? I shake my head in surprise. I search my bag for something to give him. I can only find two biros. A poor exchange, but he seems satisfied and saunters off through the trees. Tomorrow I will see the Taj, another Indian treasure, and an iconic symbol of the love of a Mughal emperor in memory of his favourite wife. But, I think it is today's gift that I will remember.

Postcard 4: The long and winding road

From Agra to Jaipur by road takes four to five long hours. The dilapidated bus is not a comfortable ride. With all its windows either broken or open, to allow a flow of air through, it rattles its way along a road with more holes in it than a slice of Emmental cheese, sloshing through the pools of water left by the recent heavy rain shower. I sit near the back and can feel the mosquitoes stabbing at my ankles. Reaching down to scratch the red bites now welling up on my feet, I regret my decision to travel in open sandals.

After the second stop for tea the road surface improves slightly. The driver, hoping, perhaps, to make up some lost time, puts his foot down and pushes his cranky vehicle to its limit. I hold on to the edge of my seat. There seem to be few rules of the road here and certainly no speed limit.

Through the dirty window I see we are travelling parallel to a wide surging river. Fed by the monsoon rains, this fat brown streak is charging along beside us in a race with our driver. But the competition is quickly over. Our vehicle suddenly crunches to a halt. The road in front of us has disappeared. The bridge that should have carried us across the river has been swept away. What now?

The driver enters into discussion with some of the passengers. The engine is re-started, and we swing off the road onto a dirt track. We take this new cross-country route for a kilometre or two, mowing down small bushes and grazing trees in our path until we come alongside a shallower section of the river.

There the bus turns. Some revving of the engine and then like a bull preparing to face the matador, we plough into the moving watery mass. I watch as the river swirls past my window and spouts up from cracks in the rusty floor, distracting the mosquitoes from their blood feast. I wonder if I am destined to drown here, never to see the pink palaces of Jaipur. But, remarkably, our unperturbed driver manages to ford the river, only causing his passengers wet feet in the process, and we continue to our destination without further mishap.

Postcard 5: I feel fine

I'm lying on the bed in a Bombay hotel room with stomach cramps. I've had this dysentery-like sickness for a few days now and feel very weak. Any further sightseeing is out of the question, as I need to be near a bathroom. I fast all day and just drink water with rehydration salts. The next morning I make my way unsteadily out of the hotel to the taxi that is taking me to the airport. It's the end of my Indian stopover. There are still several hours to go before my flight leaves, so I find a quiet corner of the airport restaurant and order the sweet caramel-coloured tea that I have become addicted to. I need to build my strength for the journey home. My muscles ache and I can feel my shoulder bones poking out from my tee shirt. I must have lost a few pounds during this trip. I look and feel unwell but hope I will make it onto the plane without attracting attention.

The waiter arrives with my tea, looks at me with suspicion and leaves without a word. I take a sip of sweet ambrosial India and hold it in my mouth for a moment before swallowing. It brings back the memory of that first taste in Agra and triggers a succession of flashbacks from my passage through India.

The call to board is still some way off, so I rummage around in my cabin bag and find what I am looking for. It's the latest gadget to hit the Japanese market, bought just before I left—my new Sony Walkman. It hasn't been released outside Japan yet, so I expect it to attract some envious looks when I arrive back in the UK. I insert a cassette tape—an old favourite, a compilation of Beatles songs. Then I lie back along the curved seat, close my eyes and press play.

See India map on page 237.

Birdsong

I turn a corner and there it is: Aureli's bar in Via Quattro Fontane, the street of the four fountains. Just a few steps away is the junction with a busy main road, which as usual is shrouded in hazy floating ribbons of sunlight intermingled with traffic fumes. A stream of dusty Fiats and whining Vespas weaves alongside the departing orange caterpillar bus that I have just stepped off. At the bus stop there is the sudden hissing release of air from another bus, as its concertina doors jerk open. Passengers spill out while new ones surge inside. Arms and bodies collide, squeezing together like pasta shapes being strained into a bowl. A momentary fusion of soft bodies in bus doorways, which is normal here; the queue is not an Italian custom. I walk on towards my destination.

As I push open the glass door of Aureli's entrance, the wafting aroma of roasted coffee beans immediately greets my nostrils. I breathe in deeply, satisfied. The bar is full of customers. Coffee is the life blood of Italian society. I am hailed from a distance by one of the barista. Very little evades the sharp eyes of Franco. He recognises me as one of the bar's regulars, a profesoressa inglese from the language school across the street. With both hands on the chrome coffee making machine, he simultaneously prepares two cappuccinos and an espresso, while acknowledging me. I feel welcome. Through the throng of people, I catch a second fleeting glimpse of Franco's starched white apron and rolled shirt sleeves as plumes of hot milk steam billow upwards. Marco, another barista, is nearby, emptying the indefatigable dishwasher, and stacking cups, saucers and glasses ready for the next batch of customers. I wade into the sea of people and ease myself through to the till where I order my coffee and pay. With scontrino in hand—my proof of purchase, I'm on my way to the counter when I recognise some of my students talking animatedly at a table in the corner. They are too engrossed to notice me. No doubt, not discussing today's homework but perhaps the latest political scandal to rock Italy. I see one of them throw his hands up in mock irony over a copy of La Repubblica, the daily newspaper. Another's face bears that 'knowing' cynical expression, which all Italians are born with.

I finally reach the counter and ostentatiously put down my scontrino, intending it to be seen. On the floor below, the first wave of breakfasting Italians have left behind the flakes of their cornetti and the screwed-up balls of their paper napkins. I wait to be served. But today the barista breezes past me to serve another. I continue waiting, trying to catch his eye. The bar is busy today. My fingers play with the receipt and, on impulse, I hold it up like a small flag. I stand like this, unnoticed, but watch as the person on either side of me is served. Frustration and then anxiety bubble up inside me. My class begins soon and there is still photocopying to do.

It's almost as if am not even here. Forgotten by the barista. The people, who were around me, are all fading away and the bar suddenly seems empty and quieter. What's that? It sounds like a bird singing somewhere. Something has happened. Perhaps it's the lull before the lunchtime rush. Surely he'll see and serve me now. He approaches at last.

My mouth anticipates the first frothy sip of a warm cappuccino. But the barista melts away behind the counter. I watch, puzzled, as his torso, then apron and gesticulating hands, mysteriously dissolve until only his face hangs wavering in front of me like a Cheshire cat. His mouth moves, voicing inaudible words. I cannot hear him but only the sound of that bird singing somewhere nearby.

The people have all vanished and Aureli's bar too. I am alone, but where? Sitting in a chair, here, in my garden. I can still hear the birdsong, but there is no one else. Recollection of the stark reality of the present floods in to fill the vacuum left in my head. I'm in a lockdown world, a coronavirus one, with its social privations. For a brief moment, my daydream transported me back to a place I inhabited some thirty years ago. A joyful dive into the rich tapestry of Italian life—close-up and personal, greeting and touching, sharing airspace, immersed in the social fabric of daily life. The antithesis of now. Now, I am alone, pondering where that world has gone and wondering if it will ever return.

See Italy map on page 240.

Senior Moments in Segovia

A high-speed RENFE train carries me calmly and efficiently into Segovia railway station. Around my sixtieth birthday an epiphany moment led first to retirement, and then brought me here. Like the younger backpacker, I am travelling to find myself—my sexagenarian self. It's also a Spanish-speaking opportunity, since I'm dutifully learning another language to keep my ageing grey matter alive.

West of Madrid, Segovia perches proud and Castilian, a rocky fortress on the Spanish plain. It's a compact city, and all roads lead conveniently into the expansive central plaza, as if to ensure that I don't miss the city's most prized asset: a larger than life second century Roman aqueduct.

In fact, I can't miss it—it's a World Heritage colossus. Twenty-eight metres high and sixteen kilometres long, it pierces the square like an unfaltering vein of granite. 'Two tiers of 167 arches comprising 20,000 stones, built entirely without the use of mortar', my guidebook informs me. The sixty-year-old in me is unnerved and surreptitiously tests it with a push. Reassuringly, it stands firm, so I sit down in a small plaza café beneath its arches to admire it some more and rest my guidebook. The camerero appears to take my order: 'Un café con leche y un pastel por favor.'

Satisfied that he has understood, I flex my weary senior feet while the Segovian sun pampers my face. I enjoy the moment, owning my time. It's a retiree's prerogative.

Afterwards, at the Aqueduct Interpretation Centre I can resume my learning, before my guidebook wills me on to follow the water's subterranean route, helpfully signposted by twenty-four pavement plaques.

Later that day, with the mysteries of Roman water engineering fully clarified for me, I ponder where next. A medieval monastery, perhaps? Or the Alcazar? Maybe mañana. After all, for a senior who is in no hurry, there is always tomorrow.

See Spain and Canary Islands map on page 238.

Maps

Japan and South Korea

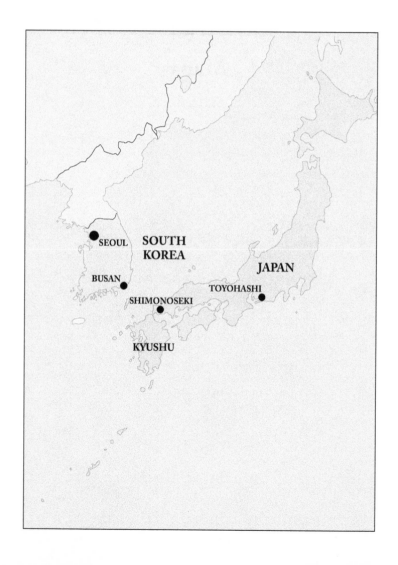

India

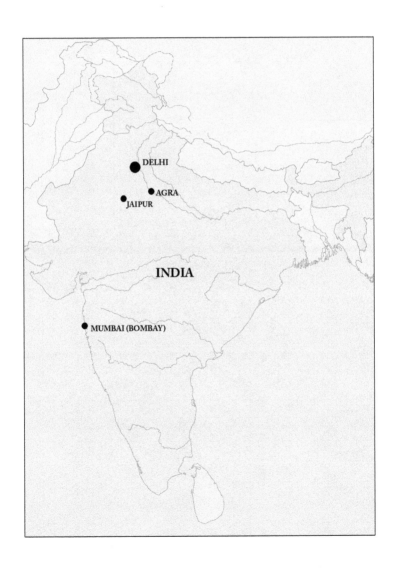

Spain and Canary Islands

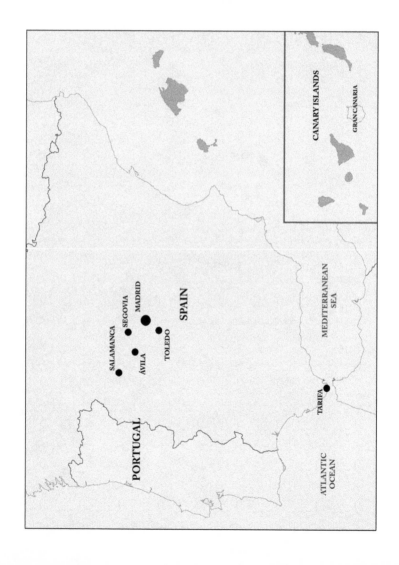

Mexico and Costa Rica

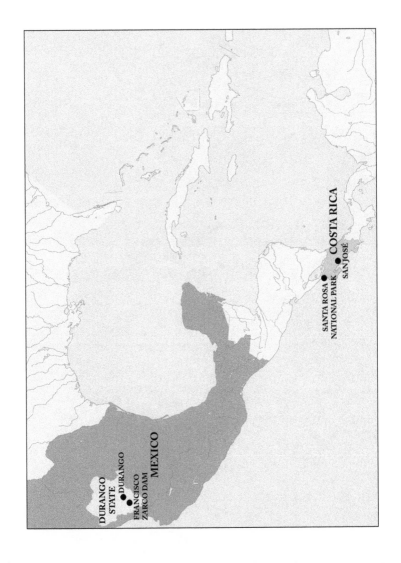

Italy

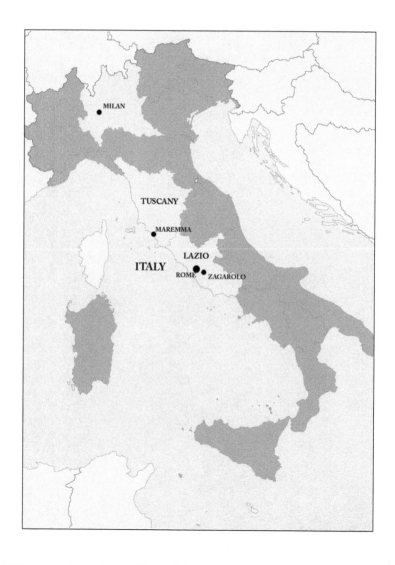

England

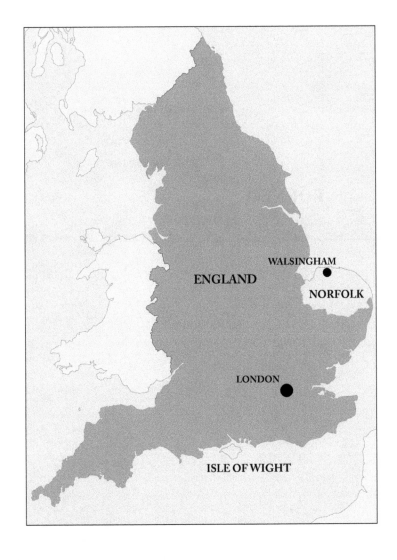

Borneo and East Malaysia

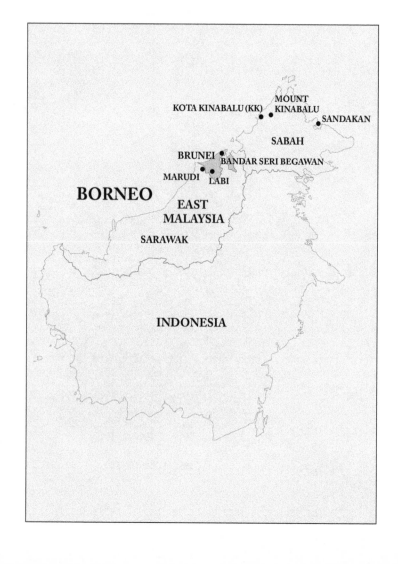

Greece, Crete, Turkey, Egypt and Israel

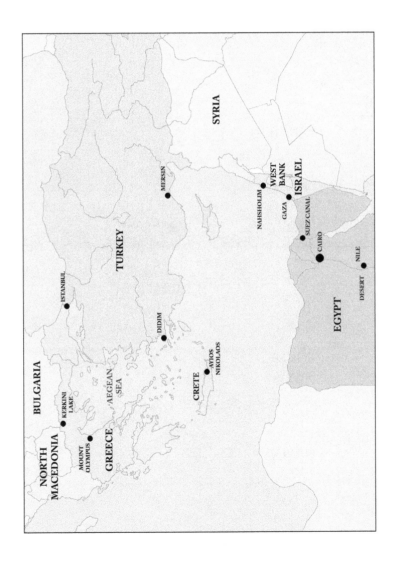

France

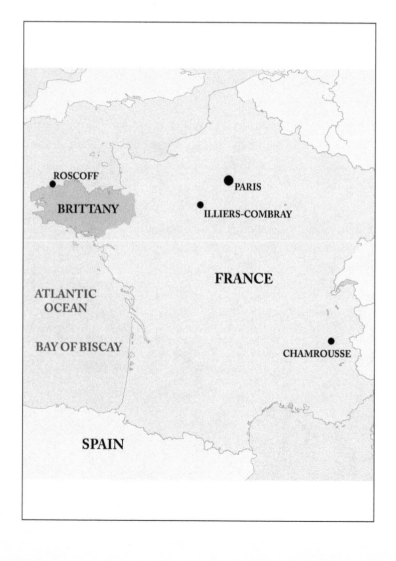

Malaysia

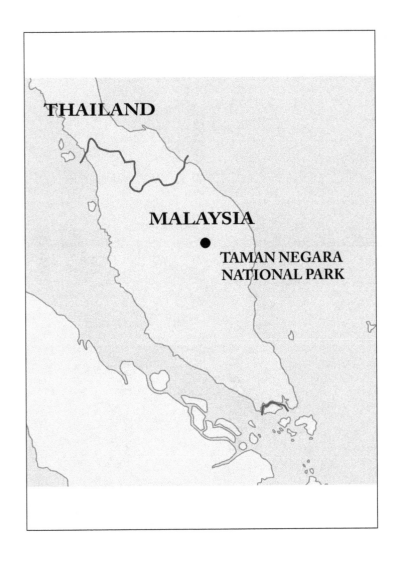

Indonesia

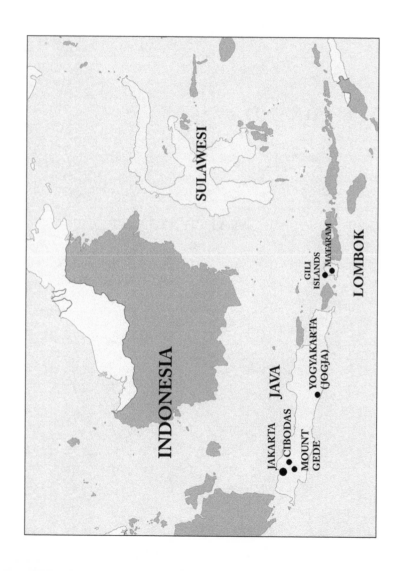

Germany, Czech Republic and Hungary

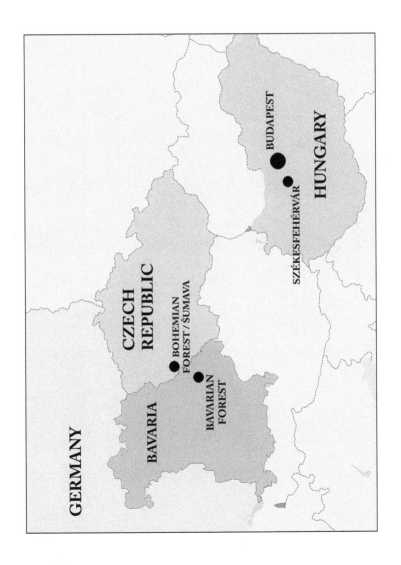

Sweden, Norway, Finland and Russia

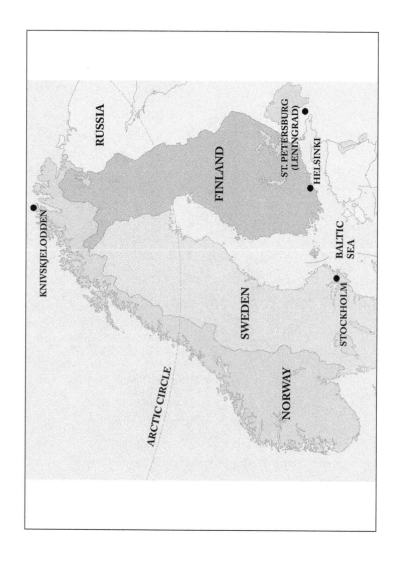